A GHOSTS OF SHADY LY NOVELLA

Long before we Lingered...

A little human child called Hapwyne stood on the knoll with her pets: a white cat, a red dog, a black horse, and a pale bird. The animals could not see Hapwyne's enemy, but they all shared her fear as a cold wind rustled the leaves on the surrounding trees.

'Where do we go now?' Asked Uimywim, the cat.
'We hide in the caves below the knoll,' replied Hapwyne.
They all agreed and followed her into the darkness.

'And what do we do now,' asked Arlyweh, the dog.
'You sit close to me and make your promises.'
They all agreed and moved closer to her.

'And after we promise?' asked Niyuwki the horse.
'You must protect me and save my humans.'
They all agreed and prepared to fight for her.

'Will *you* make a promise?' asked Tiyoawe, the bird.

Hapwyne nodded.

And the animals made their promises...

'Cats will save you from disease,' promised Uimywim.
'Dogs will protect your home,' promised Arlyweh.
'Horses will carry you far,' promised Niyuwki.
'Birds will guide you,' promised Tiyoawe.

Cat, dog, horse, and bird looked at Hapwyne.
She opened her hand.
They looked at the thing in her hand.

'What is that?' asked Uimywim.
'The Atorwitt fruit,' she said, 'I stole it from my enemy.'

'What does it do?' asked Arlyweh.
'You eat it, and it takes you where you need to go.'

'Who will eat it?' asked Niyuwki.
'We will.' Hapwyne split the fruit into five equal pieces.

'Only when you have made your *own* promise, will any of us eat that,' said Tiyoawe.

Hapwyne agreed. And as she gave each of her pets a piece of the Atorwitt fruit, she said,

'I promise that humans will always care for you.'

Satisfied with Hapwyne's promise, the animals ate up their pieces of fruit.

But Hapwyne had not told them the true nature of the Atorwitt fruit. They barely felt the pain of the poison before death took them all. And as their bodies returned to the ground, the five pieces of fruit grew as branches from their stomachs, entwined, and bound their souls to linger as eternal ghosts.

Then the tangled branches grew out of the ground,
to stand forever as,
the Twisted Tree on the Knoll.

Some believe that the promise forever binds the souls
of cats, dogs, horses, birds, and humans.
Others reason that the promise has already broken,
and now the pet begets the master's demise.

CONKER'S SIGN

Conker's Sign by L. J. Craven
Published by L. J. Craven

Copyright © 2022 L. J. Craven
All rights reserved.
No portion of this book may be reproduced in any form
without prior permission of the author.

This is a work of fiction, and entirely the product of the authors
imagination. Any resemblance to events, or to persons, or animals, living
or dead, is purely coincidental.

Cover design and illustrations by L. J. Craven

Paperback ISBN 9798841215837
Printed in Great Britain

CONKER'S SIGN published December 2022

www.ghostsofshadyly.com

This book is dedicated to anyone trying to find their way back to square one with a better bag of tricks.

Cats are not solitary. They are like us. They prefer their own company, but they still need their friends.

Fiona Best, Veterinary Technician, Ratevict.

Courage is knowing what not to fear.

Plato.

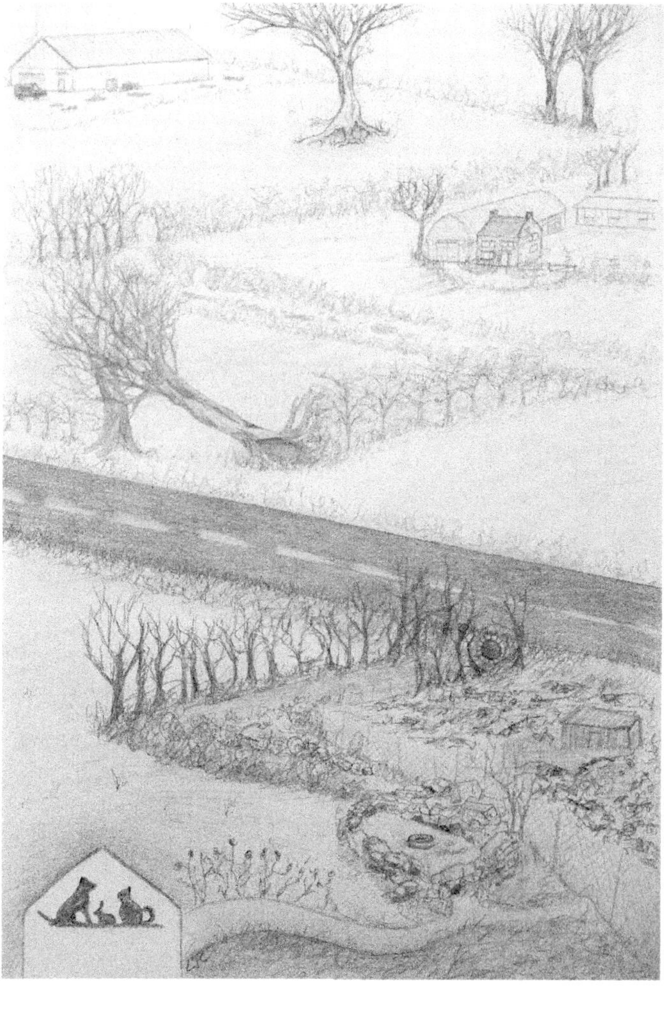

Contents

Chapter 1 - The Outside 1
Chapter 2 - The Warden of Trials 11
Chapter 3 - The Test 19
Chapter 4 - Released 27
Chapter 5 - Gone 35
Chapter 6 - The First Trial 43
Chapter 7 - Teeth 51
Chapter 8 - The Listening 63
Chapter 9 - Roads 73
Chapter 10 - The Second Trial 81
Chapter 11 - Ratters 89
Chapter 12 - The Glaring of Ghosts 99
Chapter 13 - Shadow Song 109
Chapter 14 - The Third Trial 121
Chapter 15 - Deadly Secrets 133
Chapter 16 - The Sign 141
Chapter 17 - The Trap 153

Bonus Scene - Misty 161
Bonus Scene - Winter 165
Bonus Scene - Soggy 169

1
The Outside

'CONKER! GET OUT.'

Conker dismissed Dust's warning with a flick of an ear, 'Wait ... I can see it!'

A long thin tail quivered in front of him. He stopped, held his breath, and listened. Tiny claws scraped the cold metal floor. He leant closer until he could see the rat's white rump. *There you are...* He lifted a paw.

Suddenly, a rhythmic clanging sound began echoing around the Vast Tower Box. Conker put his paw down and pricked his ears. The sound was coming from behind him. It didn't get closer. The rat didn't react. *Nothing to worry about...* He flattened his ears and bunched his quarters, ready to leap, but before he could lift a forepaw, another sound distracted him. *Footsteps...?*

'*Dontyougetnearmytruck, cat, gohuntsomewhereelse.*'

'Conker, leave it! Get out of there!'

Conker flicked his ears to Dust. 'Just a human,' he purred as he fixed his eyes on the rat's tail.

'Watch me,' Dust mewed, 'That's right human, keep your eyes on me...' Then the tabby tom yowled, 'I'VE GOT HIS ATTENTION, CONKER, GET OUT!'

Conker leapt for the rat, but just before he landed, it whipped its tail away and vanished into a gap between the full boxes. Conker swiped for it, missed, and stumbled onto the floor. Hissing with frustration, he got to his paws and pushed through the gap.

The clanging quickened, and a dark shadow fell over the full boxes around him.

'CONKER! HURRY!'

With a sigh, Conker mewed to Dust, 'I lost it! I'm coming out.' He turned and wriggled back through the gap as fast as he could, but it was too narrow for him to make it out before the last of the light vanished with a thump that rocked the floor.

The clanging stopped.

'Dust...? What's happening?'

There was no reply.

A rolling gravelly purr vibrated through the floor.

'Dust...?' Conker steadied himself as the full boxes on either side of him began to shudder and sway. A knot of dread gripped his stomach. He'd felt this before, the day he'd come to The Boxes. His skin prickled as the realisation dawned on him. *This box is moving... It's going somewhere, with me in it... It's a Moving Box...*

Conker pressed his paws firmly to the floor as it bumped and rocked. He let his body move with the swaying motion, first one way, then the other, as if he was racing around corners. Then the Moving Box lurched to a stop, making the full boxes around him shift and creak. He caught his breath, expecting them to fall. But they didn't, and as the Moving Box rocked steadily on again, its motion softened. Conker let out his breath, relaxed into its gentle rolling sway and listened as its growl quietened to a soothing rhythmic hum.

When he was sure he could walk without falling, he took a wary step forward. He could see little in the darkness and hear nothing above the relentless hum of the Moving Box. He sniffed the air. It was filling fast with a choking acrid stench, but beneath the stench, he could still detect the stale scent of the white rumped rat. *Is it still here...?* Flicking out his whiskers, he followed the scent until he found the bottom of the full boxes, and from there, he followed the scent across the floor towards the entrance. There was no way out now, just a long line of dull grey light where the rat's scent ended. He sniffed along the line. Uplifting scents flowed gently across it, just as they had done from beneath the Blue Door. *This is a door...?* He looked up and despite the darkness, he was just able to make out the edges of a large square, about the same size and shape as the square that had been high on the wall of the Vast Tower Box. *The door closed...?* With a sigh he slumped onto his belly. *The rat got out... Wherever I'm going, I'm going without food...*

Conker rested his head on his paws. Hunger gnawed at his belly, but tiredness gripped him tighter. As he yawned, his mind filled with the memory of the hunt. *Was Dust badly injured...? Did Rose catch any rats...?* He felt his eyes grow heavy. *Will Fern be okay without me...?* And as he slowly drifted into sleep, he wondered, *Will I ever see her again...?*

*

The Moving Box lurched to a stop. Conker shook the sleep from his mind and blinked open his eyes. Full boxes creaked in the darkness above him and the metal floor beneath him felt warm. The air was thick with the acrid stench. It overpowered all other scents and cut deep into the back of his throat. As he raised his head and looked around, the rhythmic clanking sound returned, and as it quickened, the line of dull grey light along the floor widened and cast aside the darkness with a bright hazy glow. Conker got to his paws and stepped back as the light washed over the full boxes and softened around him. His eyes caught movement. The door was sliding up.

Then the air moved.

Conker felt his skin tingle as moving air flooded in around him. He lifted his head high and parted his jaws as the cool air rifled through his fur and over his tongue, washing away the foul acrid stench of the Moving Box. He closed his eyes to taste the uplifting scents and flicked his ears to capture the strange sounds that it carried. Rustling, whistling, creaking... *More footsteps...?*

Conker closed his mouth, opened his eyes, and slipped back behind the full boxes. He crouched and listened as the footsteps drew near.

'*Right, whathaveigottohideforyouthistimemisterfrost,*' A human voice grumbled.

It's the same human... am I still in The Boxes...? Conker peered out from behind the full boxes. In the bright hazy light, he could see the top half of a male human in grey covers. Beyond him, shapes and colours merged into a fuzzy backdrop that shifted whenever the moving air pressed on his eyes. *It doesn't look like it...*

The full boxes in front of him began to slide forward. Conker turned and pushed through the narrow gap where the white rumped rat had been. He could still smell its stale scent as he crouched down between the last row of full boxes and the cold metallic wall behind them.

The Grey Male sniffed.

I need to move... The soft hazy light brightened, then paled to a gloomy blue as the Grey Male pulled more full boxes away and leant into the Moving Box.

'*Ohno... whatareyoudoinginherekitty cat.*'

I need to move... Conker narrowed his eyes as he looked up over the Grey Male's head. The door had rolled up above the entrance, leaving a vast open hole into an unknown world. To one side, he could see a tall grey wall with a dark floor running along the bottom of it. It looked like the inside of the Vast Tower Box, but the angles were wrong. It looked inside out. Conker blinked and turned his head. To the other side, the floor was mottled light brown with dark patches, scattered with several soft mounds that could have been crumpled full boxes. Surrounding the brown floor was an expanse of undulating green, that shimmered and swayed as it ascended into the quavering blue-grey walls. The roof rolled and rippled like soft shadowy heaps that reminded him of a cat's underbelly fur. A gigantic cat. Conker blinked. A cat that was gazing down at him warmly with one huge and blindingly bright yellow eye.

Conker flinched as the Grey Male's hand brushed his whiskers. *I need to move...*

'*Comeherelad.*'

The Grey Male's face wrinkled as it smiled around his bright green eyes, and he made a little clicking sound as he leant further into the Moving Box. *He's slow...* Conker rocked back on his haunches and with a quick glance at the mottled brown floor, he leapt. As he planted his paws on the Grey Male's hairless head, he fixed his gaze on the floor and jumped down. The Grey Male grunted and raised his arms. *Too slow, human...* Conker braced himself to land, but his paws didn't find the floor. Terror gripped him as he fell. He flicked his tail to twist his body, preparing to land, but he couldn't work out how far away the floor was. He flicked his tail again and twisted too much this time. The floor was suddenly there, and he jarred his legs as he slammed into it and stumbled heavily onto his shoulder.

'*holdonthereladcometoamos...*' The Grey Male grunted as he turned.

Conker pushed himself onto his paws, wincing as his bumped shoulder took his weight. When he lifted his head to look around, panic shuddered through him as his brain lost all sense of what he was seeing. He tried to focus on the mottled brown floor, but it crumbled into dusty clumps before his eyes, like litter that had been kicked across the floor, it darkened in the waterlogged patches. The dark floor that ran like a path around the inside out grey wall was smooth and solid looking, despite being heaped with broken and torn full boxes. Conker studied it with narrowed eyes, searching for something ... anything ... that he could focus on.

'*Thatsitstaystilllad....*'

There...! A rolling trap, identical to the ones in the Cold Box, leant against the grey wall. There was a gap underneath it.

'*Steady ... cometoamoslad...*'

Conker felt a hand brush his tail as he bounded forward and slid into the gap. The Grey Male stumbled on the litter floor and into a patch of water, landing on his hands. Mumbling angrily, he quickly got to his feet again, wiped the dirty water all over his covers, and strode towards the rolling trap.

Conker pressed himself against the inside out grey wall as the Grey Male knelt and thrust his hand into the gap. *I need to move...* He stepped back and felt the familiar soft edge of a full box. He looked round to see a pile of them, damp, crumpled, and piled against the wall. He edged back into them and folded himself into their shadows.

'*Youcantstayundertherelad,*' The Grey Male sniffed as he stood up and pulled the rolling trap away from the wall.

Conker slipped further back into the shadows of the crumpled full boxes. As he felt his eyes relax in the darkness, he carefully turned and peered out at the world beyond them. The quavering blue-grey wall had darkened into a deep indigo and the underbelly roof had dipped lower, brushing the top edges of the wall with mounds of soft shifting fur. The gigantic cat had half closed its watchful yellow eye. Without its blinding glare, he could make more sense of his surroundings. Around the edge of the brown litter floor, undulating green tendrils swished and swayed softly as they ascended like a mound of tatty covers into the distant walls. At the top of the mound, a tall dark structure stood proud on a single gnarled leg, human like, with countless tangled arms that clawed at the billowing underbelly of the giant glaring cat. Conker tipped his head. He couldn't begin to imagine what the dark structure was. It moved, yet it didn't, and in its stillness, it beckoned to him.

'*Youcommingoutoftherelad,*' the Grey Male's feet sploshed through another water filled hole as he strode back from the rolling trap and began tugging at the crumpled full boxes.

Conker backed out of the shadows and padded along the inside out grey wall. He kept his ears on the Grey Male and his eyes on the cool dark floor in front of him as he headed for the edge of the undulating green. It was closer than he'd thought, and as he stopped and sat at the edge of the brown litter floor, he could see the movement of each delicate tendril, mirroring his own long fur as they tussled and swayed in the fast-moving air.

'*Comeonlad...*'

As the frustrated Grey Male began ripping apart the pile of crumpled full boxes, Conker put a paw on the brown litter floor. He closed his eyes, lifted his chin, and let the moving air wash around his face as he listened to its gentle swooshing and whispering. *This must be The Outside ... I'm in The Outside... I'm free...* a wave of joy shuddered through him.

'*Whereareyou...*'

He opened his eyes again and stared at the tall structure. It wasn't far away. Humans were slow. If he was quick, he could scout it and get back into the Moving Box before the Grey Male had finished looking for him. He raised his head as he took a step forward, and sniffed the moving air, relishing how it enlivened him as it flowed through his fur.

'*Heyohnoyoudontkitty cat...*'

I need to move... Conker let the air pull him forwards and push him onwards towards the tall structure. Its bracing freshness strengthened him, washed away his fear and powered up his paws. He walked slowly at first, apprehensive of his first steps, but his pace hastened with every uplifting breath, until he was trotting, then running over the brown litter and into the soft green waves of the undulating green.

'Ohno ... thereyougo, thereyougo ... goodbyekitty cat.'

The swaying tendrils felt cool around his legs. He pricked his ears and let them follow the sounds of The Outside. A cacophony of unfamiliar noises whistled and waltzed around him. He leapt towards them and bounded up the slope. *Move...* The air lifted his fur and moved him on, faster and faster, over the green and up towards the tall structure. He'd never run so fast, never stretched his muscles so far. *Move...* He raced on, his paws thrumming the tangled floor until it gave way to a soft dusty brown.

Then the air softened, slowing him gently and bringing him to a stop in the shadow of the tall structure. A fierce rustling, silent but deafening, lent a constant background to eerie creaks and groans as he stepped cautiously towards its one gnarly leg. Ceaseless chirrups and cheeps echoed melodically from every corner of the blue grey walls. He let his ears follow the sounds, trying to make sense of the overlapping, wrangling tunes.

Digging his claws deep into the dusty brown floor, Conker looked up into the countless wavering arms of the tall structure above him. As he watched, mesmerised by their movement, a drop of water fell onto his nose. He gasped, then licked it away. Then another fell onto his back, making him shiver from head to tail. He tasted the air again. A myriad of uplifting scents grazed his tongue. He recognised none of them, but he savoured them all. *The Outside...!*

With a deep sigh, Conker slumped down at the foot of the tall structure. He rested his head on his paws and closed his eyes. He was hungry and exhausted, but he purred, letting his breathing slow as he listened to the sounds cavorting around him ... the swooshing of the moving air ... the rustling of the tall structure's arms ... the crunching of dusty floor close by... he flicked an ear. *Paw steps...?*

Then a voice.

'Don't ... move!'

2
The Warden of Trials

A cat...? Conker lifted his head and tasted the air. He quickly found the scent of a tom cat, laden with fear, excitement, and damp.

'Don't move...' the tom repeated, 'Don't come any closer!'

'Who's there?' Conker looked around. Not too far away, a little black and white tom peered up at him from behind one of the tall structure's gnarly feet. He was half Conker's size, terribly thin, and the white patches on his damp fur were tinged with green. As he gazed at Conker with one wide rheumy eye, his head tilted as if he hadn't the strength to lift it. His other eye was closed tight inside a large red bump. Conker's jaw dropped. *What happened to this cat...?*

'You ... don't know who I am?' The little tom's good eye widened as he stared up at Conker, 'You were sent to find me, yet you ask who I am?'

'I wasn't sent to find you, so how *would* I know who you are? I've never even been here before.'

'Is there a White Kitten tugging my tail?' the little tom mewed.

'What?' Conker could taste the little tom's overpowering fear scent as he leant closer and peered over his back, 'I don't see one.'

'You are Uaelmyst, aren't you?'

'I missed what?' Conker glanced back at the Moving Box.' It was still there.

With his good eye trained on Conker, the little tom shuffled forward and sat up stiffly, 'You are Uaelmyst, the Night Cat, aren't you? You have been sent by Uimywim to those she will not meet. You've come to drag me into the Ether?'

'No, I'm Conker and I came from The Boxes.' Conker sat up tall and dipped his head, 'What happened to your eye?'

The little tom shuffled back awkwardly as Conker drew himself up to his full height. 'My eye is fine.'

'The other one.'

'I only need one eye to see the truth!'

Conker tipped his head, puzzled by the tom's awkward way of moving, 'Are your legs okay?' he mewed kindly.

'Yes, they are. Who are you really?'

'Are you stuck?'

'No, I am not. Answer the question.'

Conker shook his head, 'What question?'

'Who *are* you?'

'I just told you; I am Conker.'

'Just Conker? No Mother Name?' the little tom narrowed his good eye, 'A huge cat like you must have a Father Name too.'

'My name is Conker, just Conker.'

'Is that so...?' the little tom slumped back down with a sigh, 'Then what are you doing here, Conker, just Conker?'

Conker looked back at the Moving Box. It sat motionless beside the inside out grey wall. The sliding door was still up, and a few full boxes remained inside. There was no sight or sound of the Grey Male. *I still have time...* He turned back to the little tom, 'I'm just scouting this place.'

The little tom shook his head awkwardly, 'So, you came from a box? What box? Where?'

'The Boxes. I don't know where they are,' Conker shrugged. 'It's a human place and I was inside it.'

'But you got out?'

'Yes, I got stuck in that Moving Box over there.'

'Moving Box?'

Yes, that...' Conker flicked his tail, 'over there next to the inside out grey wall.'

'That's a truck.' The little tom sighed. 'You got in a truck?'

Another drop of water fell on Conker's back. He stretched his head over his shoulder to sniff it. As he did, it rolled down his fur and dripped onto the floor beside him. He watched it soak away into the dusty brown floor, then he turned back to the little tom, 'This is The Outside, isn't it?'

The little tom looked up again, 'Yes ... we are outside.'

Conker gazed up into the outstretched arms of the tall structure above him. They were barely moving where their thicker ends joined the gnarly body, but the thinner, outermost arms whirled and waltzed with one another to the tune of the fierce moving air. And yet they were so calm and still. The soft furry mounds on the underbelly roof rolled motionlessly above the arms before scudding away into a distant yet exact same place. The indigo walls shifted away whenever he tried to focus on them, but never ceased to enclose him, trapping him in the growing red glow of the gigantic cat's bright glaring eye. Conker shivered.

'You've never been outside before?' the little tom shuffled closer and parted his jaws to take in Conker's scent, 'Are you testing me.'

'No, I'm not.' Conker shook his head as he failed to follow the fall of another drop of water.

'You have tufts on your ears.' The little tom mewed.

'I ... what?'

'Tufts, and marks.'

'What marks?' Conker tipped his head.

'The dots in your ear.'

Conker flicked his ears. He had no idea what this cat was talking about. 'there's nothing wrong with my ears.'

'No cat I've ever seen before has tufts and dots.'

Conker watched another drop of water land, and soak away into the dusty brown floor. 'I've never been here before...'

'So, you said.'

'It was an accident,' Conker explained. 'I was hunting rats with my friends, and I got trapped in the Moving... the truck.'

'Your ... friends?' the little tom flicked his ears nervously.

'They're not here,' Conker dipped his head and mewed gently, 'My friends are all still in The Boxes. But, if The Outside is good for hunting, I will tell them about it when I get back and bring them with me next time...' he paused as the little tom's good eye went wider, then went on, 'There are nine of us, and we are all big. But if you tell me your name, I will tell them you are a friend.'

'How do you know I'm a friend,' The little tom asked as he ducked down awkwardly behind the gnarly foot. When he reappeared, he held something that looked like a badly chewed piece of the tall structure in his jaws.

'What's that?' Conker glanced at the swaying arms above him.

'It's a magic stick. It banishes the things I don't like. So, don't touch it!' The little tom growled as he bit down hard on it.

Conker glanced at the Truck again. 'Okay,' he mewed, 'It was nice to meet you, but I have to go.' He got to his paws and turned to leave.

'WAIT!'

Conker paused.

'I am a keeper of secret knowledge.' The little tom pushed his stick aside with a grunt and tried to sit up tall. 'If you want to know my name, you should tell me about your friends, and where they are,' he flicked his tail to the truck, and winced as it flopped weakly to the side.

Conker gasped, 'What's wrong with your tail?'

'Tails lie, you should listen to my words,' the little tom crouched down clumsily and manoeuvred the magic stick between his paws, Conker noticed that he was also missing most of his claws. 'Now, tell me about your friends.'

Conker sat down and waited until the little tom had his teeth firmly clamped into the magic stick again, then he began. 'The humans call us Ratters. I am the biggest, but we are all closer to my size than yours. Violet and Rose are sisters. Violet is a sweet natured cat, but Rose has a temper. Then there is Briar, he's a big tom with strong opinions and hairbrained ideas, but he's ok. Dust is almost as big as me.

He's a good cat, and smart. Gloworm is...' Conker chose his words carefully, '...a little strange, but very observant. Spinney sees the fun in everything, he even likes Ratbots! Onyx is smart and mysterious. And then there's Fern, my closest friend. She's kind and beautiful, but nervous... And what happened to your claws?'

The little tom let go of the stick, 'I lost my claws defending the secret knowledge. What's so special about Fern?'

'I promised to keep her safe. She relies on me, and I don't want to let her down.'

'So, you want to get back to her?'

'Yes, I do.'

'There's only one way to get back to her now.'

'Yes, I know. In the truck.' Conker got to his paws again, 'Which is where I'm going now.' He turned and began padding back towards the undulating green.

'How do you know it will go back to The Boxes?'

Conker froze.

The little tom crunched his teeth into the stick.

Conker turned back. 'What do you mean?'

'I mean, that you are in terrible danger and only I can help you now.'

Conker let out a deep sigh and looked back over his shoulder at the little tom. 'I'm not in any danger. I can get back in that truck before you're on your paws and I will be back in The Boxes before you get across the ... green stuff.'

The little tom shifted awkwardly, 'I don't doubt your strength and speed, Conker, but get back in that truck at your peril! Even I won't be able to save you.'

'Save me from what?' Conker glanced around The Outside. *From what...?* The tall structure swayed softly above him. Little glistening drops of water patted lightly onto the dusty floor. All around them, tangled green tendrils flailed merrily in the gentle moving air. The quavering walls had darkened as the one bright eye of the gigantic cat began to dim and close as the underbelly roof rolled on. He had no idea what he was looking at, but nothing felt dangerous. The only danger he was in was missing the truck.

'From your death, and a certain meeting with The White Kitten.'

Conker shook his head. 'Goodbye,' he mewed kindly, 'it was nice to meet you.' Then he turned away and started padding back to the undulating green.

'STOP!' the little tom yowled, 'I will not let you do this. You are a good cat, and I will save you.'

Another drop of water fell onto Conker's back as he turned and glared at the little tom. It ran deep into his thick fur and made him shiver. The little tom pushed his stick aside with a paw and hauled himself onto his shaky legs. Conker's stomach knotted as he noticed how frail he appeared, how he struggled to push himself up with his hind paws, how his tail flopped limply onto the ground, and how he dragged himself forward clumsily with one foreleg raised as panic widened his one good eye. His fear scent was stifling. *Could there be danger I can't sense...* A gust of moving air rattled the outstretched arms above him. *What do I know about The Outside...?* A flurry of drops smashed into the floor around him. Green tendrils flailed as the quavering walls billowed and darkened, and an eerie glow seeped from under the dimming bright eye and tinged the underbelly roof in a deep blood red. *I don't know anything...* With a deep sigh, Conker padded back to the gnarly feet and sat down heavily, 'Okay, I'll listen.'

'Thank you ... you ... you will thank me! You have made the right choice.'

Conker's paws tingled uneasily as he watched the little tom drag his stick to his side and shuffle uncomfortably towards him, 'Is there something wrong with your front leg too?' he asked.

The little tom purred, 'I'm saving my energy to save you.'

Conker shook his head.

'And help you get back to Fern.'

'What's wrong with the truck?'

'The trucks are controlled by humans. The humans could take it anywhere, maybe somewhere you have no chance of ever returning from?'

'The Grey Male,' Conker glanced over his shoulder, 'He will recognise me. He knows where I came from.'

'But sometimes, humans take cats to other places. Dangerous places. Do you understand the danger you are in now, Conker?'

Conker hung his head. It wasn't long since he'd been bundled into a trap and taken to The Boxes. He'd known then that he'd never see his siblings again. *What if he's right about this truck...?* 'Okay,' he mewed, 'No more nonsense. Just tell me who you are and how I can get back to Fern?'

The little tom blinked his good eye and nodded slowly, 'My name is Soggy. Kii'pip Romi, Soggy, and I am the Warden of Trials.'

3
The Test

'Soggy?'

'Yes,' Soggy bowed, gracelessly.

'Warden of Trials?' Conker tipped his head to one side, 'What does *that* mean?'

Soggy raised his paw and licked the sore toes where his claws had been. 'It means, that I am warden of the territory known as *The Trials.*'

'And where's that?'

'I'll tell you when you pass the test.'

'What test?' Conker sighed.

'A test to find out who our friends really are. If you pass, you will find your friends.'

'What if I don't?'

'The Warden of Trials is fair. I will wait until you do.'

'And, what happens when I pass?'

Soggy lowered his paw, drew his magic stick to his chest, and leant closer to Conker, 'I will tell you about The Trials. The Three Trials that you must pass if you are to find The Sign. The Sign that you need to find, to find your friends.'

'Okay, you're not making any sense. I really am going now.' Conker got to his paws. But as he turned around and took a step forward, another cold drop of water landed on his back. His legs froze. *That doesn't make any sense... Why is water falling from the roof...?* He closed his eyes and lifted his chin to let the moving air rifle through his fur, it felt good. *But why does it move...? That doesn't make any sense...* He flicked his ears to the swooshing and rustling around the motionless outstretched arms of the tall structure. *That doesn't make any sense....* He opened his eyes and gazed around at the dark quavering walls, and then up at the mounds of fur on the underbelly roof that rolled on and on above him, illuminated by the blindingly bright eye as it slowly closed, casting The Outside into blood shadows. He tried to take another step forward.

'At your peril ... Conker ... just Conker.'

Nothing in The Outside makes sense... Conker turned back to Soggy. 'Okay, I'll do The Test.'

'Good choice, now listen closely. I will only say this once.' Soggy shuffled himself into the best sitting position he could manage and raised his head. Then, with a painful sounding cough to clear his throat, he mewed in a slow, dramatic voice:

> *'I will alert your friends to my greatest need,*
> *'As I growl when things are not in my favour.*
> *'But fill me not with your speed or your greed,*
> *'I'm appeased only by something you savour.'*

'What?' Conker mewed.

Soggy sighed and repeated the riddle.

'Ok, what do I do now?'

'Solve the riddle, then bring me your answer to pass the test ... I'll wait here.' Soggy slumped down with a grunt and bit down hard on his magic stick.

Conker sat down and watched Soggy as his breathing slowed, his head flopped to the side and his stick fell from his jaws. When he was sure the little tom was fast asleep, he mulled over the riddle. *Greatest need...? Growl when things are not in my favour...?* He tried to think of the greatest need that he'd had in The Boxes. *Staying together, no ... I've trained alone ... that's not it. Water...? No, there's always water. Ratbots...?* He shook his head and purred. *No ... I never needed Ratbots! only the food I got when I caught them...* Conker licked his lips as he remembered the last bite of warm rat flesh that he'd eaten, and his stomach growled. *Growl...! That's it...!* Conker leant over Soggy, and whispered into the sleeping tom's ear, 'Easy! The answer is stomach. You want me to bring you food. Wait here, I will be right back.'

But as Conker padded to the edge of the undulating green and looked around again. A frightening realisation clawed at his empty stomach. *The riddle was easy ... but how do I find the answer...?* He had no idea where to start looking for food.

Another drop of cold water landed on his back, then another, and suddenly, water was thudding to the floor all around him, each drop bigger than the last as they thumped into the soft green tendrils and exploded. Then they hit him, harder and harder, slithering down into his thick black fur. *How can I hunt in this...?* He parted his jaws to try and find a single scent that he could follow, but as the falling water wrestled with the moving air, all the scents wafted together, until he couldn't tell one from another. Water ran into his ears, and into his eyes. *I can't do anything in this...* Conker shook away the water and leapt back into the shelter of the tall structure.

Soggy pawed at his stick and mumbled in his sleep.

'Soggy?' Conker leant towards the little tom, 'can I ask you something? Before I bring you my answer, can I ask you a question about The Outside?'

Soggy slowly opened his good eye, 'You can ask. I will know if you're trying to cheat.'

'Okay,' Conker flicked the gnarly leg of the tall structure with his tail, 'I just want to know what this is?'

'This?'

'This tall structure that we're under. With this thick leg and twisted feet ... and all the outstretched arms up there.'

Soggy purred, 'You mean a tree.'

'A tree...?' Conker stared up at the hypnotic swaying above him. *Gloworm's Mother Name... Seek dreams in the trees... Gloworm doesn't even know what a tree is...*

'A Tree,' Soggy yawned. 'It grows from the ground to provide shelter and it cleans the air.'

'I can see how it's a good shelter,' Conker dug his claws into the dry floor beneath his paws as he watched the water flooding the ground a few paces away, 'But how does it clean the air?'

Soggy purred, 'The tree's leg is called a trunk and its *arms* are called branches. They grow leaves ... see those flappy bits at the ends?'

Conker nodded.

Soggy went on, 'The leaves beat the foul smells from the air. That makes them turn brown, and when they are fully brown, they crumple and fall off. Then the tree sucks new life up through its roots ... these,' he tapped the gnarly foot with his paw, '...and new leaves grow on the branches to beat the air again.'

Conker narrowed his eyes to focus on the rhythmic flapping of the leaves. *That makes sense...* 'And the air,' he asked, 'Does it move because of the leaves?'

'Because of the wind. The relentless invisible force that hunts the air.' Soggy swayed his head clumsily from side to side. 'The air is lazy. It likes to be still and full of stench. But the wind does not like this, so it stalks the air, slowly, guiding it towards the leaves. But if the air refuses to move, the wind gets mad and howls, and leaps after it, knocking down and flinging aside anything in its path as it hunts it down. And when the wind catches the air, it hurls it into the leaves, to be beaten ... into fresh patches.'

'Fresh patches...?' Conker parted his jaws and sucked in the air around him. As it filled his lungs, it filled him with energy. The air inside The Boxes had never felt like this. 'I can taste them...' he purred, turning his head from side to side as he drew in another breath, 'I can taste the fresh patches.'

Soggy blinked and rested his head back down on his paws.

'So, that's what's making the rustling noise? The leaves beating the air?'

Soggy nodded.

'And the other noises? The chirping and cawing ... is that the tree too?'

Soggy purred, 'That, Conker, is the birds. They are nothing to worry about. All you need to know is that we eat them...' he raised his voice and yowled, 'THEY DO NOT EAT US!'

A frantic flapping sound caught Conker's ears. He looked up to see a dark figure thrash its long flat forelegs clumsily in the branches before it lunged up into the underbelly roof, circled awkwardly, and soared away. 'Is that a ... bird? Why are its legs flat...? How do they stay up...?'

'Wings. Those flappy forelegs are used for flying in the air instead of running on the ground. Watch out for that one, the one with the broken wing. He looks like trouble.'

Conker watched the bird go, then as if by magic, he saw them all. Hundreds of little black shapes gliding and swooping, spinning, and soaring in and out of the soft mounds of fur as they scudded across the underbelly roof. A few settled in the branches, then took off again. One dove into the undulating green and folded its wings as it landed. Conker extended his claws and pushed them down into the dusty brown floor as he watched the bird's wings vanish into its sleek body. As it scuffled around in the green tendrils, Conker's stomach rumbled, but before he could take a step forward, the bird took off again. Conker watched it go, then looked back at the undulating green. 'And that floor ... the green?'

Soggy half opened his good eye. 'Grass. It grows from the ground like the trees. It is food to some creatures, and a home to others?'

'What is it to us?'

'A soft place to sit mostly,' Soggy purred again, 'but it's good to hide in and chewing the blades can remove bits of food from your teeth.'

'And this brown floor, it's soft, and crumbly ... why?'

'It's the earth,' Soggy raised his head again, 'The great collector. When it collects the warmth of the sun, it becomes dry and warm and good to lie on. When it collects the cold, it freezes solid. And when it collects water, it becomes slippery and perilous to cross. It collects the fallen leaves from the trees, and it collects the dead. Everything that has ever lived will one day become part of its collection.'

Conker shivered as he dug his claws deeper into the dusty surface of the earth. It was dry and warm. 'The sun? what's that?'

'That,' Soggy flicked at ear to the blood-streaked bright glaring eye, 'is the sun. The Mother's Eye. She blinks slowly as she leaps over the world, scattering the shadows and the cold and the damp with her bright fierce glare, opening the flowers, and raising the mists to make ... warm places for her kittens to sleep.'

Conker closed his eyes and faced the sun. He was impressed at how it warmed his face. 'And the water ... why does water fall from the roof?'

'Rain. You can curse it for the discomfort it brings, most cats do, but it also brings life. And it takes life too if you are not careful. Water is as sly as a snake. It is still when cold, but when it is warm, it slithers back up into the clouds.'

'Clouds?' Conker looked up, 'Those fluffy mounds that look like belly fur?'

Soggy nodded, 'As our mother's belly bought us milk, the clouds in the sky give us rain. The sky is cold, so it cools the sly water to stop it moving and throws it back down again ... because we can't drink it up there.'

'Thank you,' Conker purred. He felt a pang of warmth for the little tom. *Perhaps he's not so bad after all...*

He waited while Soggy repositioned his stick, bit down on it, closed his eye, and drifted back into a peaceful sleep. Then with his head high, he set off again through the long, wet grass in the falling rain. As he walked, he breathed in the fresh patches of air, and he felt his stomach grumble in time to the chirping of the birds. *Food is the answer to the Test ... I will find this cat some food...*

4
Released

Conker's thick black coat melded into the shadows as he stalked through the long grass, and the rain eased into little light drops that pattered gently along his back. He paused to lap one from his shoulder, amazed at how he could drink from his fur. *No need for water bowls in The Outside...!*

He stopped at the edge of the brown litter floor and reached out a paw to touch it. It looked and smelt like litter mixed with earth. *Litter earth...?* Not wanting to think about why the earth would want to collect litter, he turned his attention to the rolling trap and crumpled full boxes by the grey wall. *It's not inside out...* Conker thought, *It's the outside of a box... A huge Grey Box...* The Moving Box stood motionless beside it. *It has feet... round rolling feet, like the rolling traps...*

The Grey Male was nowhere in sight, but as Conker flicked his ears to the wall of the Grey Box, he heard muffled human voices. *He's not the only one here...* Conker tasted the air. All traces of human scent had been washed away by the rain, but the smell of their food was strong in the air.

The chatter of the birds and the whooshing of the wind filled his ears as he hopped out of the grass, bounded across the litter earth and dived under the rolling trap. But as

Conker pushed his way further into the shadows, the sounds of The Outside were swept aside by the dull monotonous hum of The Boxes, a sound so familiar, he'd never even noticed it before.

With his ears trained on the human voices, Conker slid from under the rolling trap and crept along the dark floor towards the end of the grey wall. When he came to the truck, he paused to sniff the air around it. The acrid stench had faded where the rain had washed over its smooth white shiny body, but it was still strong in the shadows below its belly. The voices were louder here. Conker slipped under the belly of the truck and crouched behind its round black foot. From where he sat, he could see around the corner of the Grey Box to where a slip of yellow light fell from a door and pooled across the dark floor.

Conker slipped out from under the truck and padded cautiously around the pool of light. When he reached the door, he peered through the gap. Rows of silhouetted towers stood in a dim yellow light between him, and a half open brown door at the far end. He closed his eyes as he tried to remember the towers in the Vast Tower Box, where he'd hunted with Dust and Rose not so long ago. They had been so tall they'd vanished up into the gloomy, unseen roof. He opened his eyes again. The towers in this box were shorter and narrower, their tops visible below the dark grey beams of a sloping roof. Heaps and piles of tangled and twisted human objects, bulged, and drooped from every ledge, some he recognised, but many of the shapes were new to him.

The stench of human food clung to the stagnant air as Conker slipped through the door and slid into the shadows of the nearest tower. He slowed is breathing as he padded cautiously along the bottom of it, and out into the open space towards the brown door. His skin tingled as the muffled human voices grew louder, and as he reached the door, his fur was on end. A male human he'd never heard before was talking to The Grey Male.

'Whatdowehavetohideformrfrostthistime.'
'Moreblackboxesofdead rats whydoeshewantthem.'
'Neveraskamos, neverask.'

Conker let his ears follow their voices as he peered around the brown door. The small box behind it was crammed and cluttered with full boxes, bowls, sweepers, and soft covers. His fur flattened as he recognised these objects, and their faint familiar smell of sour damp.

The Grey Male was sat at a high ledge, rummaging around in a shiny white cover. Conker recalled its sound from the larger black covers Fiona had used to clean the litters. He could just see the legs of another male human sat opposite him. Conker raised himself onto his hind legs to get a better view, just as the Grey Male pulled a long pale object out of the shiny cover, similar in size to his own fingers, but mushy and floppy. Conker gasped as the Grey Male ate it. He'd never seen humans eat anything like that before. The revolting stench that drifted from it turned his stomach, but somewhere within that foul smell, he detected the fleshy aroma of something more like food. Somewhere in that shiny white cover, there was something that Soggy could eat.

'Hasthatkettleboiledyetamos, dyingforabrew.'
'Iwillgoandcheck.'

The Grey Male stood up and moved around the high ledge. Conker kept his ears trained on him, ready to run if he came too close, but he went through another door at the back of the box, uttering in a voice so melodic and distracting, that Conker didn't see the other human stand up.

'Anyplatesandforksinthereamos, chipsarefullofgrease.'
'Someupinthatcupboardithink.'

Conker watched the other human as he sidestepped around the ledge. His scruffy brown covers were as ill-fitting as the Grey Males', and his thick brown head fur was as fluffed as a frightened kitten. As he joined the Grey Male in the box beyond the other door, Conker saw his chance.

Easy...

He slipped into the box, trotted across the floor, leapt up onto the high ledge, and peered into the shiny white cover. A hazy warmth surrounded his face as the stench of human food clogged his nostrils. All he could see was a putrid mass of floppy fingers, but he could smell something edible. He reached in with a paw and pushed the fingers aside, and was surprised when they revealed a long, shrivelled, black and brown object. Conker dug a claw into it, pulled it towards him and sniffed it. It smelt like moist dry nuggets. His stomach began to growl, and he remembered Fern's words, *"I didn't know there was any other food, where ... what does it come from?"*

'Ohnowhatareyoudoinginhere.'

Conker shook his head to clear his thoughts and clamped his teeth into the food, gasping as it oozed a sizzling and surprisingly tasty liquid. It reminded him of hot and stale rat flesh.

'Getoutofit cat.'

Through a hole in the white cover, he could see the Grey Male standing in the doorway carrying two drinking bowls. He'd seen them before and remembered that the humans needed to put them down before using their hands. He had time to get away. But as he began to move, the shiny white cover moved with him.

'Hey, notmysausage.'

As the Grey Male stepped forward, Conker stepped back, ready to leap for the door. But as he turned, his hind paw slipped on the edge of the ledge, and he fell. The cover fell with him, showering him in a stinking mass of greasy fingers. The Grey Male put the drinking bowls down. Conker shook himself, trying to get free of the cover, but all he did was spread the mass further across the floor.

'Whathappenedamos.'

'The cat thatescapedfrompmd, itjustknockedthechips everywhere.'

I can't lose this... Conker sunk his teeth deeper into the food as he backed away from the humans. A greasy lump squelched beneath his paw. He slipped again, and the cover slid further down around his neck and tightened as he looked around for the door.

'Hemustbehungrytocomebackinhere.'

'Welltheynevergotfeddidthey, nowhesgotmysausage.'

Conker dragged the cover with him as he backed out of the door. It flapped around his legs as he moved, slowing him down. He tried to duck under it, but it twisted again and rode up over his face. He didn't see the tower before he crashed into it. Full boxes wobbled and brightly coloured coils tumbled to the floor around him. Conker clawed at the cover and shook his head, trying to free himself, but it just fell further over his eyes.

'Chasehimoutbeforehewreckstheplace,'

As Conker hit another tower, footsteps moved towards him. He tightened his grip on the food, and as the cooling juice ran down his chin, he closed his eyes and held his breath. Moving air ruffled his tail. *The door to The Outside is behind me...* The footsteps came closer. He took another step back, but as he tried to turn towards the door, the cover snagged on something unseen and pulled tight around his neck. He snatched at it with his claws, trying to cut himself free, but he couldn't get a hold on it, and it just twisted tighter and tighter until he couldn't breathe. The footsteps stopped. He gave the cover one big tug, but his paws slipped, and he fell heavily onto his side.

'Dontmovelad.'

Conker tried to get up, but the cover was choking him. His paws couldn't find their grip on the greasy floor. He couldn't get his breath. *I can't move...* He sunk to the floor and closed his eyes.

'Thatsitstaystill.'

Conker heard a click, and his neck was tugged upwards. His head swayed for a moment before it was lowered gently back down to the floor. He gasped. Fresh moving air filled his lungs. *I can breathe...* As he raised his head, the cover fell away, and he was looking up into the bright green eyes of the Grey Male.

'Getoutofherekitty cat, keepthesausage, andgofind yourselfafarmtoliveon.'

Conker held the Grey Male's gaze as he slowly got to his paws. Careful not to slip on the greasy floor, he stepped backwards around the fallen objects and over the last lumps of mushy fingers. Then, when he was certain that the humans weren't going to stay where they were, he tightened his grip on the food, turned, and bounded for the open door.

'Goodluck, cat.'
'Yeahgoodluck, betteroffoutthere.'

Conker dived back under the truck and collapsed behind its round black foot. He dropped the food and panted for breath. He was alive and he was in The Outside again. Cold drops of rain crashed into the litter earth around him. He could feel the spray landing on his fur and trickling down onto his skin. He lapped at his shoulder. The cold rain cooled the food juice in his mouth and made if feel uncomfortably sticky on his teeth, but his stomach growled after its lingering taste. *I'm hungry... But I'm not starving...*

As Conker looked back at the tree in the distance, he made his decision. Humans were slow. He had time to take the food to Soggy and say his goodbyes. The little tom had a point, but he was sure the humans and their truck were perfectly safe. They were his only way back to Fern. Once Soggy had food, he would climb back into the truck and wait until it returned him to The Boxes, *Then, I'll tell Fern and the others all about The Outside...*

5
Gone

'Soggy?' Conker dropped the food by the tree roots. *Where is he...?*

The wind whipped the air through his fur as he raised his head and looked around. The sun had fallen from the sky and sat glumly in a distant pool of gooey yellow light, like a kitten who'd toppled her milk bowl. Deepening shadows slithered away from her, through the grass, up into the trees, and melded into the walls. And above the walls, the clouds billowed, black and bloodshot as they bunched together and hurled the rain back down to the earth. Even in the shelter of the tree, the air felt cold and damp. Conker shivered as he licked the stale, sticky food juice from his jaws, then he sniffed the air. The dull ache of hunger gave way to the grip of panic as his eyes widened to the dark desolate emptiness of The Outside, and the realisation that there was no longer any trace of the little tom's scent. *He's gone...?*

The rain roared and smashed into the ground around the tree as Conker circled the trunk, sniffing the earth for any remaining remnant of Soggy's scent, but he found nothing. He lifted his head again, taking a deep breath as he looked out into the creeping darkness. He could see the truck, bright white and glimmering as torrents of water washed over its smooth body. *Did he follow me...?* Conker shook his head. *No, I'd have seen him on the way back...* The rain cascaded from the roof of the Grey Box and washed over the crumpled full boxes and the rolling traps against the wall. *Unless he's hiding...?*

Bracing himself, Conker leapt forward, bounded into the battering rain, and raced back across the sodden grass and the waterlogged litter earth towards the grey wall, certain that Soggy must be hiding under the rolling trap, watching him. But as he dived into the gap again, he smelt nothing except the musty damp of the crumpled full boxes. Soggy wasn't there. Conker sat for a heartbeat and listened to the soft human voices behind the wall, barely audible above the incessant hum of the Grey Box. *He's not here...* He tasted the air again as he looked out from the gap. The truck sat motionlessly nearby. *I still have time to find him...* Conker slipped out from under the rolling trap and raced back through the rain towards the tree.

As he reached the tree, he shook out his wet fur and parted his jaws. The food hadn't moved, but its scent had weakened. He sniffed around it and froze as he found a faint trace of Soggy's scent. *He is here...?* He raised his head and flicked his ears but found no sight or sound of the little tom. Picking up the scent again, Conker followed it to where Soggy had been sleeping, and from there, he followed it to the edge of the grass. *Why did he go this way...?* The scent was faint in places and stronger in others, so Conker lowered his nose and followed it carefully through the grass. The fresh smell of rain and the strong scents rising from the wet earth made the trail hard to follow, but he could tell there was something odd about it. It wasn't like the scent trail left by a cat walking. It was as if Soggy had not walked but dragged himself on his belly through the grass. *Dragging himself where...?* He looked up, and through the falling rain he could just make out a distant line of small trees in the farthest corner of The Outside.

Conker growled with frustration. Certain that the little tom must be hiding in the small trees, he hurried down the grassy slope towards them. But the far corner was further away than he thought. He quickened his pace but was no closer to the line of small trees when the last trace of Soggy's scent faded away. Shuddering with cold, Conker stopped and sniffed around. He found a myriad of other smells, but Soggy's scent had gone. He turned and padded back through the sodden earth to the tree, keeping his head low and his jaws open. The long grass tickled his nose and whipped his eyes as he tried in vain to relocate the scent.

He found it again under the shelter of the tree. Confused, Conker shook more rain from his soaking fur and turned to follow it in the opposite direction. Only now, the scent trail zigzagged all over the grass, as if Soggy had been trying to get away from something. Conker stopped and lifted his head to look around the darkening emptiness of The Outside. *From what...?*

The riling wind took a deep breath and drove the air up around him. The leaves on the tree above him thrashed it back down through his fur. Conker shivered again as the wind whistled and howled. He pricked his ears. *What was that...?* His fur rose along his spine as the wind howled louder with an enduring, forlorn voice that stole his breath away. Panic gripped him in the eerie quiet that followed. 'Soggy?' Shaking, he turned and raced back to the tree.

Ducking down into its roots, he hissed, 'Soggy? Where are you?'

The rain stopped falling as quickly as it had started, and the wind retreated to let the fresh air rest amongst the leaves. Conker raised his head and looked back across the grass towards the line of small trees in the distance. The far corner looked even further away now. *The Outside is growing...?* he shook his head and looked at the sky roof. He couldn't tell where it joined the wavering walls. The bright orange clouds had slipped so far down them, making the edges of The Outside hard to decipher. *How will I find him if everything keeps changing...?*

I will find him... Conker took a deep breath and got to his paws, then padded back across the grass to the last place he'd smelt the little tom's scent. He tracked it, and this time, it led away in another direction, spiralling out around the clumps of long grass, then meandering down the slope towards another far corner where two tall trees swayed side by side. He followed it, quickening his pace as the wind took a deep breath, and as the two trees in the corner began to slip further away, the wind raised its voice and howled again.

Conker froze, held his breath, and listened. *It's speaking... The wind has a voice...?* The long slow yowl, cat like, yet not like any cat Conker had ever heard before, faded away as he let out his breath and gazed around. The Outside was still. Nothing moved. But everything was moving. The wind moved the grass and the leaves and the trees, the rain fell and splashed, rippling the water on the floor. His wet fur lifted and fell, the black and bright orange clouds scudded across the indigo roof and the sun snuck further down into the earth. And as he gazed around, the distant corners of The Outside slid further away from him. Conker lowered his head and sniffed the earth around his paws. Soggy's scent had vanished again.

With his ears pricked and his jaws parted, Conker turned and headed back up the slope to the tree, one steady paw step at a time. In places he was sure he could smell the little tom, but his scent trail was broken up by the strong scents of the earth. *Does the earth collect scents too...?* He padded around the roots of the tree. The food was still there, cooling and congealing, it didn't look as appetising now, even though it's stench still made his stomach growl. *How do humans eat this...?* He looked at the Grey Box. The truck sat still in its lengthened shadows. Then he looked at the line of small trees, silhouetted against the wavering indigo walls. They were no longer in a corner. He blinked. The two swaying trees in the other far corner were even further away, and their corner had gone too. Conker felt his eyes widen as he gazed around him. *Where are the corners...?* There was no line where the wavering walls joined the sky roof. Everything was melding and expanding outwards, like the thoughts in his mind. *The Outside is not a box...! It's everywhere...!*

Conker sat down heavily and closed his eyes. And when he lifted his head and opened them again, he saw tiny specks of bright light twinkling in the darkness all around him. glimmering from where the walls had been, shining from where the roof had been, flickering between the rolling clouds, glistening down at him from the farthest reaches of his vision. Hundreds of them. So high up, so far away. He tried to fix his gaze on them as he circled the tree.

The wind rose gently and followed him, teasing him as it ruffled his fur and rustled the leaves above him. Then it whistled around him, lifted the last of the dry dust from the roots, and offered Soggy's scent again.

'Where are you...?' Conker padded away from the tree, but as soon as he reached the grass, the little tom's scent vanished. *The earth...? has the earth collected Soggy...?* He felt an icy shiver run down his spine. He'd followed the little tom's scent to the corners of The Outside, and now the corners were gone. Only the sun remained as a distinct sinking dome in the distance. *The Sun...* Conker turned and looked at the arc of light beyond the edge of the undulating grass. *I didn't look there...*

'SOGGY!' he yowled as he bounded across the grass towards into the warmth of the falling sun. As he ran, the rain spiralled and spat at him and the wind lifted and raced with him, down the slope towards the deep twisted shadows and the last of the blood red light. 'Soggy...?' The wind rose and roared in reply, then it howled. *That's not the wind... that is a voice... There's something hiding in the wind...*

Conker stopped. *Something dragged the little tom in circles through the grass...? Something took Soggy, like the earth takes scent...* Something howled again. Conker shivered. *Something's hunting cats...*

A clanking sound rose through the air. Then a bang rang out and echoed around him, clear and crisp above the whistling and wailing and howling of the wind. *The truck...* Conker spun around and raced back towards the tree. Bright lights flashed towards him, forcing him to slow his pace and lower his eyes. A low rumbling growl drowned out the receding wail of the wind. Conker kept his head low as he quickened his pace again. *It's going...*

The bright light swung away across the grass as Conker passed the tree. He stopped at the edge of the grass and watched in horror as the truck trundled around in a circle, then rolled away from the Grey Box and into the shadows of the distant trees. *It's gone...*

Conker hung his head. The wind gently caressed his fur, and the rain pattered softly along his spine as he padded back into the shelter of the tree. *Now I'll never see Fern again...* With a deep sigh he slumped to the ground.

Soggy purred as he shuffled awkwardly from between the tree's roots and put a shaky paw on the food. 'Well done, Conker,' he mewed, 'you have passed the test.'

6
The First Trial

'The truck has gone!' Conker growled.

'You made the right decision,' Soggy purred.

Conker flopped down by the roots of the tree and dropped his chin onto his paws. *I'll never get home...* Despite the heat of his anger, a cold shiver ran through his body and seeped into his bones. He tore his gaze from the little tom and looked up into the tree. The sky that billowed above the swaying branches, had turned a menacing deep blue. The tiny glimmering lights twinkled weakly, illuminating nothing. A solitary beaten leaf fell from its branch and spiralled downward on the gentle wind. Down to the earth. Down to be collected. Gone forever. *Like Fern...* Conker extended his claws and dug them into the dry crumbly ground. He liked the way his claws slid so easily into it, and he relished its gentle resistance, as if it was allowing his anger to grow as it dragged him down into its collection.

'Would you like some sausage?'

Conker shook his thoughts away and blinked at Soggy, 'Like ... what?'

'This...' With a shaky paw, Soggy pushed the chewed lump of food towards Conker. 'This is called a sausage. One of the best human foods you can get. They rarely share these with cats. You did well to get it.'

Conker sniffed, 'I nearly got caught.'

'But you didn't.'

'I wish I had. If I'd been caught, the Grey Male would have taken me back to The Boxes.'

Soggy pulled his magic stick towards him. 'Are you sure you were nearly caught? Didn't the Grey Male let you go? Perhaps he wanted to set you free.'

Conker shook his head. *He's wrong... Why would a human want me to be free...? I'll never see her again...* Fern's words crept back into his mind as the smell of food crept back into his nose. *I didn't know there was any other food, where ... what does it come from....?* His stomach growled as he leant forward and sniffed the sausage.

'I don't know where they come from,' Soggy shook his head, 'but I do know I can't eat it all myself, and you must be starving by now. So, eat, while I tell you about The Trials.'

Conker reached out a paw and dug a claw into the sausage. The little tom had managed to eat over half of it. *He must have been starving...* His anger faded as his stomach dropped like a stone. *He did need food... and I helped him get it...* With a sigh, Conker pulled the remains of the sausage towards him, took a small bite, and began to chew. He wasn't sure his stomach was ready to be filled with food again, but its grumbling eased as he worked the spongy morsal around in his mouth. It was more tender and tastier than he'd expected, and as he swallowed, he began to understand why humans were reluctant to share them.

'Good, isn't it?' Soggy purred.

Conker nodded as he took another bite. Then another. His hunger waned with each mouthful, but as his stomach filled, so did his mind. *How can I get back to Fern...? The truck had gone... How can I sit in a patch of fresh clean air, under a tree, and eat sausage in The Outside while Fern is forced to hunt the vicious rats in The Boxes...? How...?* A thought occurred to him while he chewed... 'Soggy?' Conker swallowed and looked up, 'If this is your territory, you must know when the truck comes back.'

Soggy sighed, 'This is not my territory. I am the Warden of Trials. The Trials, and the secret knowledge they bestow upon any cat who passes them, that is my territory.'

Conker blinked, 'And where is that ... exactly?'

Soggy straightened himself up as well as he could and tried to lift his chin, 'It's not a place, it's a journey.'

'A journey ... to where?' Conker gazed around.

'The Sign.'

'What sign?'

'The Sign that you need to find to find your way back to your friends,' Soggy mewed wistfully,

Conker shook his head, 'And where is it?'

'The Trials will take you to The Sign.'

'Are you sure?'

'Not yet,' Soggy tried to shake his head, 'But a cat who passes the test will always be successful in finding The Sign. That, I *am* sure of.'

Conker twitched his whiskers, 'And I'm sure that the wind has thrashed the sense out of your ears.'

Soggy's good eye glimmered as he purred, 'Then we better get started before the same happens to you. I feel the wind picking up again. Are you ready for the First Trial?'

Conker took another bite of the sausage and nodded. He had no idea what this cat was going on about, or even what a trial was, but this little tom was clearly very determined to tell him. 'Okay,' he swallowed, 'I'll be ready for the First Trial, after you tell me when the truck comes back.'

Soggy dug his remaining claws into the magic stick and hung his head, then he mewed sadly, 'I have never seen a truck return to this place. If you want to see your friend Fern again, your only hope is to complete the Trials and find The Sign.'

Conker blinked, 'Never?'

'In all the time I've been under this tree, I have never seen that truck, or any other truck, go away, and then come back.'

Conker closed his eyes and sighed, 'Then I guess I'm ready.'

Soggy nodded, 'Walk with me.'

Conker opened his eyes again and watched with concern as Soggy picked up the magic stick, bit down hard on it, and dragged himself awkwardly to his paws. Then he padded clumsily towards the grass on three stiff legs, one forepaw raised, and his bent tail dragging listlessly along the floor.

Certain that the little tom was going to topple over as the floor became more uneven, Conker hurried after him, ready to duck under his shoulder if he began to lean too much. Soggy stopped next to a large clump of grass, sat down awkwardly, and dropped the magic stick. Then he raised his head, stared up at the tiny twinkling lights with his one good eye and flicked an ear to a patch of dusty floor beside him, inviting Conker to sit.

Conker sat and waited for Soggy to speak.

'In passing a simple test, Conker, you have proven yourself capable of true friendship. You decided to help me and forgo the truck. It was a wise choice, for only I, The Warden of Trials, can help you get back to your friends.'

'So, where did you go?' Conker mewed, 'When I came back with the sausage? where were you?'

Soggy mewed, 'I never went anywhere.'

Conker rolled his eyes, 'You were nowhere to be seen. Your scent was all over the place one moment and gone the next. And what was howling? It sounded like a voice in the wind. I thought something had hunted you down and taken you for their meal?'

Soggy sniffed, 'The wind carries many voices. They are of little concern for cats. The Trials are your concern now.' He lowered his voice, 'But, be warned. The Trials are not as simple as the Test. Even the First Trial will be taxing for a strong and brave cat like you. Now, are you ready, Conker, just Conker, Ratter of The Boxes, pilferer of sausages, and avoider of trucks, to begin the First Trial?'

Conker dug his claws into the damp earth and glanced back at the dry patch of litter floor where the truck had been. *What choice do I have...?* 'Okay,' he growled, 'let's do this.'

Soggy cleared his throat, and meowed:

'Your journey begins,
'To carry me far away,
'As you walk alone.'

'What does that mean?' Conker looked around. The wind howled through the leaves above him, but kept its voices hidden.

'Solve the riddle to begin the First Trial.'

Conker watched Soggy struggle to grip his magic stick in his teeth. It was covered in bite marks, and he wondered what was so magic about it, but he didn't dare ask, he wasn't sure he wanted to know the answer. So, instead, he resigned himself to solving the riddle. *Your journey begins ... to carry me far away ... as you walk alone... Easy...* 'I've got it.'

Soggy dropped his stick and flicked and ear, 'Already?'

'Well, it's obvious. '*Your journey begins*, means we start a journey. And *to carry me far away,* means that I will go far away and, *as you walk alone,*' Conker tipped his head to one side, 'Wait ... what do you mean walk alone? Do I have to go alone?'

Soggy slowly lifted his paw and licked it.

A knot of dread gripped Conker's stomach. He looked at the little tom's foreleg. A patch of missing fur exposed the swollen red skin beneath it, and flecks of dried blood surrounded his sore toes where his claws had been. He took a deep breath, 'You can't walk far, can you?'

Soggy shook his head.

Conker sighed, 'But how can I go on any journey alone? I don't know anything about The Outside. I don't even know what The Sign is.'

'But you must find it, Conker. It's the only way back to Fern.'

Conker thrashed his tail. The cold wind ruffled his fur and stung his eyes as he gazed up at the twinkling lights. *What are they...?* He looked across the wavering grass. The distant trees were black against the indigo sky, and beyond them, mounds of earth rolled on forever. Only the static Grey Box was familiar in the shifting landscape of The

Outside. Even with Soggy's explanations, he still had no idea what he might find out there, or how to deal with it. He knew rats and he knew boxes. That was all. *But I must do this...* He took a deep breath and let the billowing wind flow over his tongue and fill his lungs, filling himself with the anticipation of a journey into the outside. Into the unknown. *I can do this alone...* Full of the refreshing air, he puffed out his chest and raised his head. As the wind buffeted against him, he felt strong. Stronger than Soggy. *Strong...* he looked down at the little tom, so frail and bent out of shape that the wind rocked him on his paws. *He can't walk... he can't hunt...* Conker sighed. *I can't leave him here alone...* then an idea struck him, 'Wait,' he mewed, 'that wasn't the answer, was it?'

Soggy lifted his head and blinked his good eye.

'You *are* coming with me,' Conker purred. "To carry me far away". You said that, so it means that *I* carry *you*! So, *I* will walk alone, with *you* on my back. And that way, you can direct me to The Sign.'

Soggy rested his chin on his stick and sighed, 'Thank you...'

'And I can hunt for us,' Conker leapt to his paws and paced around Soggy, 'so we will eat well. And you can tell me more about The Outside on the way.'

Soggy looked up at Conker. His good eye twinkled as he mewed, 'Then let us begin your first trial.'

7
Teeth

Conker pressed his belly to the ground and took a deep breath. He didn't want to get this wrong. If he dropped Soggy, he was sure the little tom would break.

'How did you get so big?' Soggy groaned as he slid his good foreleg over Conker's back.

'I'm not big,' Conker purred, 'Well, okay, I am the biggest Ratter, but we are all about the same size.'

'I've never met another cat as big as you,' Soggy slipped his sore foreleg over and lay down lightly across Conker's back, 'all the cats I've ever met are closer to my size than yours.'

Conker turned his head slowly. The little tom had sunk almost completely into his thick black fur, his forelegs barely reached the bottom of his rib cage and his head rested comfortably behind his shoulder. 'So, all cats in The Outside are small?' he asked.

'You're a big cat, Conker. I am glad you are not my enemy.'

Conker purred. 'I'm no cat's enemy.'

Soggy sighed, 'Good, let's keep it that way... I think I'm ready now. Please pass me my magic stick?'

Conker looked at the heavily chewed stick by his paws and gave in to his curiosity. 'Why do you need it?'

'Because I...' Soggy lifted his head from Conker's shoulder fur, 'Because the trees carry wisdom, and I, as a keeper of secret knowledge, like to carry trees.'

Conker purred as he reached out a paw and slid the stick toward him. *That's sounds like nonsense...* Steadily, he bent down and grasped the end of the stick in his teeth, turned his head, and passed it back to Soggy.

Soggy gripped it tight in his jaws, 'Tank Koo,' he mewed around it.

'Not a problem, Conker purred. 'So, where to?'

'Do vem Dwees.'

Conker looked at the two swaying trees in the distance.'

'Dod vem, ve uber onvs.'

Conker looked at the line of small trees at the other end of the grass.

'Yef, vem onvs.'

'Do you want me to carry it for you? I could use some wisdom.'

'Doh!' Soggy shuffled about on Conker's back, 'No... I can carry it like this.'

'Good, because I don't want to get lost,' Conker could barely feel Soggy's weight on his back, and his remaining claws barely scratched the skin beneath his thick fur. 'Hold on tight,' he mewed, 'and don't worry, your claws won't hurt me.'

Soggy purred again as he dug his claws a little deeper into Conker's fur.

Conker lifted his rump first, then his shoulder's, and slowly stood up.

'Your fur reminds me of a thick warm bed, I'm sure I'll sleep well on our journey.'

'Don't sleep too deeply, I don't want to forget you're there and drop you.'

'Please don't do that, it's a long way down.'

Conker purred as he took a tentative step forward. It took a few steps to get his balance, but after that, carrying Soggy was easy. The little tom stayed still and hung on just tightly enough. Conker found his stride and set off down the slope of swaying grass towards the line of short trees and the shadows that stretched out beyond them. The earth beneath the long grass felt soft and damp, and pleasantly cooling on his paws. The rain had eased into a sparse soothing spray and the wind rippled his fur gently as he walked. He lifted his head and parted his jaws to taste the scents it carried. Fresh sharp smells mingled with earthy aromas that lifted his spirits.

Conker slowed as he neared the edge of the grass. The long, twisted mass of tendrils and leaves that crossed the ground before him looked as though something had ripped apart a tree, chewed it up and spat it out dead into the shadows. He flicked his ears to the wind and shivered.

'That's a hedge,' Soggy mewed, as if sensing Conker's uneasiness. He lifted his head a little and explained, 'It's made of very small trees and big spiky plants. But don't worry, it is nothing that will harm us. We only need to be afraid of what might be lurking within it.'

Conker gasped, 'Like what?'

'Like other cats,' Soggy purred as he dropped his head back down into Conker's fur.

'I don't mind meeting other cats,' Conker mewed. *Even crazy ones...* He flicked his ears again but herd no voices in the wind this time. He'd become accustomed to the sounds around him now. The quietly deafening rustle of the leaves on the trees had faded into the background. The incessant chirping and cawing of the birds had settled into a delicate twittering melody. Not a sound came from the shadowy hedge, so he padded forwards and sniffed along the soft green leaves that dangled from its outermost branches.

'There is a hole just over there,' Soggy mewed, 'it's big, so you will be able to walk through it easily.'

Conker spotted a well-trodden trail a few paces away. It ran over a rise in the bare brown earth and through a hole in the hedge. 'Is that the right path?' he flicked his tail towards it.

'I hope so,' Soggy purred.

Conker took a deep breath as he stepped onto the path and padded up the rise. The hole was almost big enough for a human to crawl through, and as he peered into it, he could see another hedge not far away. Between the hedges lay a stretch of litter floor, not unlike the one next to the Grey Box, only here it had more pools of water and was strewn with large odd-shaped objects and remnants of trees and leaves. It didn't look safe to cross, but Soggy remained still on his back. *He'll tell me if there's danger...* Conker stepped down from the rise and gasped as his paws sunk into icy cold bubbling water.

'Steady,' Soggy grappled with the stick and dug a claw into Conker's ribs.

'Water! lots of it.' Conker scrambled back up the rise and shook out his paws.

'It's a brook, nothing to worry about. Very useful if you need to drink or look for fish.'

'Brook?' Conker stared into the channel of water hidden beneath the long grass.

'The brook is safe ... it is the thorns in the hedge you should worry about.'

'Thorns?' Conker peered into the hole.

'The teeth of the hedge. Sharp enough to tug out your fur and rip your flesh if you go too fast ... but harmless of you keep your pace steady.'

'What?' Conker shook his head.

Soggy sighed. 'The brook isn't too deep and it's safe to walk through,' 'But go carefully through the hedge.'

Conker stepped warily into the icy water of the brook. Then he stopped. *Brook...* 'My teeth!' he gasped, 'Now I remember! It's what Brook said when I lost my teeth!'

'Your teeth? A brook said what?' Soggy mewed.

'I'd almost forgotten what she said...'

'Is the wind getting in your ears?'

'Now I know I'll find Fern...'

'I'm sure you will.'

'I know I will,' Conker took a deep breath, 'Because of what my friend Brook told me.'

'Brook is a friend? A cat?'

'Yes, she's a cat. And the only friend I ever had in The Old Place.'

'Well, I'd love to hear what she said,' Soggy mewed, 'But let's walk while you talk. The shadows are starting to steal the warmth from the world.'

'Where do I go? There's no hole in the other hedge.'

'Follow the path down towards the last of the sun's light. 'It's a bit muddy, so stay in the middle where it's higher and drier.'

'Muddy?'

'Mud. It's what you get when the earth collects too much water. Dogs like playing in mud but mud is not for cats.'

'Dogs?'

'A rare beast, nothing to worry about.'

Conker nodded. He looked at the path beyond the hole, 'Why does the earth keep water in those pools?'

'Puddles. It's the water waiting to be collected by the earth. Walk carefully around them.'

'And those lumps everywhere, what are they?'

'Pebbles, stones, rocks, boulders. They have many names. They are the most ancient, and greatest part of the earth. They don't collect water and they don't turn into mud. So, they are very good for cats. It is said that the White Kitten has her own rock in the Void in the Fold. Some even call her Pebblepaw and believe that she made the world with a pebble and a pool of her own tears.'

'So, I can walk on them? Conker nudged a large stone with his paw.

'Best not to, they wobble.'

Conker twitched his whiskers, 'Middle bit it is then.' He stepped carefully through the hedge and out onto the soft, muddy earth. The sodden ground squelched through his thick fur and up between his toes as he padded into the middle of the path. He was glad of the firmer ground there, but the mud still clung to the fur around his paws.

The last of the sun's blood red light was receding over the undulating grass in the distance, casting everything around them into gentle silhouettes. As his eyes adjusted, Conker set a steady pace along the rough path, and began to tell Soggy his story.

'Brook was the first cat I met after my brother and sister were taken away. I was very young, and I'd only just learned how to sleep without Acorn and Petal beside me. I was still too small and too slow to catch Ratbots. But I was determined to catch every single one. So, I concentrated on running faster and faster, until one day, I caught one. I remember how I leapt and stretched out my legs as far as I could, and just managed to dig a claw into the tip of its tail. Then I swiped it into the air and when it landed, I span it around and sunk my teeth deep into its crunchy back. It hurt my teeth, but the Ratbot stayed still. The humans bought me food as a reward, and they combed my fur. That night, as I licked the remains of the food from my aching teeth, I felt like a real cat. I slept well, and my dreams were the most comforting I'd ever had.

'But when I woke the next morning, something was wrong. As I sat up and began to groom, my mouth felt strange. A ripple of dread followed my tongue along my spine, all the way to the knot at the end of my tail. When I tried to grip the knot with my teeth, my teeth were not there.'

'None of them were there?' Soggy raised his head.

'Well, all of them except my four long teeth. The teeth I'd used to defeat the Ratbot the day before. The important ones. They had gone. I looked everywhere for them. They were not in my bed, or on the floor or tangled in the covers. They had vanished.' Conker sighed as the memory of his despair clouded his mind. His paw caught a stone and he stumbled. 'Sorry ... are you okay there?' he mewed as he steadied himself.

'I'm fine, just go steady and keep talking. I think I'm going to enjoy your story.'

Conker found his footing and set off again, keeping his eyes trained on the path ahead so he could avoid the stones and puddles, he went on; 'When the humans took me back to the Turn Box, I searched for my teeth, but they were not there either. I felt so miserable I hid under a ledge and tried to sleep, hoping that they would be there when I woke. But the humans wouldn't let me sleep. They just kept on crashing their Ratbots into me.'

'What *exactly* are Ratbots?' Soggy mewed.

'It's shaped like a rat, but smaller than a real one. And it's fast with round whizzy feet instead of legs. The humans control them. If we catch them, we get food.'

Soggy purred, 'I think I had one of those once. I didn't bother catching it, so I didn't get any rewards. Not sure what happened to it... anyway, don't let me interrupt.'

'Then you know how annoying they are.' Conker purred, 'Well, I gave up. I couldn't hunt without teeth, and I didn't want to chase them anymore. I didn't even feel like a real cat—'

Conker slowed his pace. The hedge beside him had thinned and through its sparse branches and leaves, he could see a vast open space with an undulating floor of ridges and trenches that rose gradually into the distance. At the top, darkened against the blood red light of the vanishing sun, he could see a cluster of huge, crooked boxes. The leaves along the hedge rustled in a wave as the wind hastened. A hidden voice howled.

Soggy prodded Conker with his stick, 'It's a farm. Nothing to worry about.'

Conker pricked his ears and let them follow the wind. He could hear a faint howling, and in that eerie howl, he was sure he could hear words. Not the words of any language he'd heard a cat speak, but not much different. He felt Soggy tense on his back. *Something's there again...* 'What is that howling?' he asked.

'Farms make strange noises. We are safe on this path, but we should keep walking. Before the shadows steal any more of the light.'

The forlorn voice wailed with the rising wind as Conker set off again. He kept his ears trained on the farm and his eyes on the path ahead of him. *He's right ... the shadows are taking everything...* It was getting darker. Sticky mud clung to his fur, and despite the warmth of Soggy's body over his back, the cold of the earth crept deeper into his bones. His teeth began to chatter.

Teeth... 'I didn't find my teeth...' Conker continued his story, '...and I didn't catch the Ratbots. I was afraid that I might die of hunger and as the humans grew more and more frustrated with me, my rewards shrank into smaller and colder piles of food. I hid under the ledges every time they took me to the Turn Box and refused to chase anything. They stopped grooming me and started ignoring me.'

A howl drifted above them on the whistling wind. Like the yowl of a cat, but this was no cat. The voice was too low, and it was close.'

'Just the farm,' Soggy shivered, 'Keep walking ... keep talking.'

Conker nodded and trudged on through the muddy shadows. He didn't feel safe. Every hair on his body whispered to him, *run away... run away...* But he had to go on. He took a deep breath, let it out slowly, and carried on talking. 'Then ... one day, when I was hiding under a ledge, the humans brought another cat into the Turn Box. She was older than me, with sleek brown spotted fur and a long stripy tail. Her name was Brook. I remember how she purred gently as she crawled under the ledge to greet me, then she curled up beside me and asked me why I was hiding, why my little eyes were so full of sorrow and why there was so much fear in my scent.'

The wind heaved and thrashed the air through the leaves along the hedge. Something thrummed across the wet earth on the other side of it, getting louder and closer. Soggy took a deep breath and held it. Conker felt his fur rise along his spine.

'Keep walking, keep talking,' Soggy mewed quietly as he let out his breath.

'I ... I curled up in Brook's paws and ... I told her all about losing my teeth,' Conker tried to ignore the sounds in the wind as he went on, 'She groomed my fur as she listened to my story, and when I'd finished telling it, she told me something I will never forget.'

'Tell ... me,' Soggy mewed.

'She told me, *'If you ever lose anything dear to you, keep a door forever open in your heart, so it knows it will always be welcome back.'*

The thrumming quickened on the other side of the hedge. Conker glanced through it but saw nothing.

Soggy shivered and mewed, 'I like that... Go on...'

'I never saw Brook again,' Conker continued, 'but I thought about her words every night ... and as I slept, I imagined opening a door in my heart and wishing for my teeth to return. Then one day I woke to an agonising pain in my jaw ... And as I ran my tongue over my painful swollen gums, I found the tip of a tooth. They had come back. Brook was right. My teeth had come back! bigger, and stronger than before. And then I knew, that thanks to my friend Brook, I will never lose anything I love again.'

Something splattered through the mud along the other side of the hedge. Conker caught a new scent, but the wind hurled it into the leaves and thrashed it away before he could decipher it.

'If you found your lost teeth, Conker, I have no doubt that you will find the cat you love.'

'I will find her. There is nothing...' He flicked his ears, 'Nothing that can stop me...'

'Then don't stop now! Let us get to The Sign, quickly!'

The wind howled. Something sniffed. A stick snapped.

'Keep walking...' Soggy growled, '...and keep your eyes on the earth.'

'What ... is it...?' Conker felt his words stick in his throat. Something was moving towards them. He could feel it. But he saw no movement in the dark shadows. He could hear something. *Breathing...? Panting...?*

'Keep your eyes down,' Soggy growled.

Conker looked up as the hedge in front of him shifted and swayed. And his eyes went wide as a huge white beast crashed through it with a terrifying snarl. Its hairy body blazed in the shadows as it growled and loomed closer. Conker could not take his eyes off it. Terror tore at him, but he stood his ground. Soggy shivered in his rising fur. *I won't let it hurt him* ... Conker curled his lips and hissed. *I need him...*

And the beast lunged, parting its slavering jaws to reveal huge, white, glistening teeth.

8
The Listening

The shaggy white beast edged closer, snarling, and spraying spittle as it gnashed its teeth. Conker hissed and held its gaze as he stepped back. He could feel its breath, riling the fur on his face like a hot angry wind. He could feel Soggy shifting on his back. *Stay still...* Conker willed the little tom. It was up to him now. He had to get them away from the deadly beast. 'Hang on tight,' Conker mewed, 'we need to run...'

'Don't Run!' Soggy growled, 'Stand still and lower your eyes.'

Conker braced himself and lowered his eyes until he could see the long black claws on the monster's huge hairy paws, but he couldn't stop his gaze from traveling back up its long shaggy legs and over its powerful shoulders. He saw it drop its haunches. *It's going to pounce...* He pressed his weight into his hind paws, ready to turn. 'Hold on Soggy... we need to run ... Its hunting us...'

'No! She isn't. let her come forward.'

'What?' Conker stepped back. 'Look at its teeth ... look at its legs ... it's going to leap...'

'She won't! Stand still!' Conker felt Soggy poke him in the ribs with his stick, 'You need to trust me. Lower your eyes and let her come closer.'

Conker shook his head. He'd never seen a monster so big and ferocious. He wanted to run, to get them both away. *Can I get away...? If I run, this beast will outrun me ... Soggy will fall ... it will eat him ... I'll never find The Sign....* Conker took a deep breath. He had no choice but to trust him. The little tom knew The Outside. He didn't. He dug his claws into the muddy earth and dropped his gaze to the floor.

'Thank you.' Soggy mewed.

Conker kept his eyes trained on the beast's huge paws as they stepped closer. He could smell its breath, strong and laced with the fleshy scent of food. *It's already eaten...* Conker held his breath as it growled and moved forward to sniff his muzzle.

Soggy dug a claw into Conker's ribs, raised his head, and meowed, 'Still your jaw and sway your tail, so Red Wind can hear *our* tale.'

The beast clamped its jaws shut and took two steps back.

Conker raised his eyes a little and watched, fascinated, as it sat down heavily in front of him and looked up into the sky. Then it thumped its hairy white tail three times on the floor and woofed, 'Let the Red Wind rest tonight.'

'Back up a bit and crouch down,' Soggy mewed, 'She needs space to lie down too.'

'What is she?' Conker mewed as he stepped back and lowered himself carefully to the floor.

'She's a dog.' Soggy dropped his stick to the ground, shuffled backwards and slid from Conker's back. 'I told you dogs are nothing to worry about. She seems very friendly.'

Friendly...? Conker shook his head as he watched Soggy limp painfully around him, pick up his stick and flop down in front of the dog. *I have so much to learn about The Outside...*

Soggy dropped his stick again, 'Hello,' he mewed, 'My name is Kii'pip Romi, Soggy, and this is my very big and strong friend, Conker... He has no Mother Name, he escaped from a human box, and he has never been outside before, so ... please, excuse his manners.'

The dog stretched out further across the floor, unbothered by the puddle that she dragged her belly through, nodded to Soggy, and barked, 'I am Winter, Ffar Fuyhiwwf.' Then she looked at Conker and tipped her head to one side, 'I see you are marked. Were you a prisoner of the humans?'

'I don't know,' Conker tipped his head. *Does she mean my ears...?* 'I'm from The Boxes.'

Winter tipped her head the other way and raised an ear, as if awaiting more information.

Conker went on, 'I'm a Ratter. Humans took me to The Boxes. In The Old Place we chased Ratbots for food. But now we must catch rats and turn them into food. I escaped in a truck and then I escaped from that and now I am here ... trying to get back there...'

Winter nodded, 'So, you control the rats in human places. Just as I protect the sheep in their fields. You fulfil your promise as I fulfil mine,' she scratched her ear with a hind paw as she studied Conker, 'I would welcome a big strong cat like you in my barn...' she glanced at Soggy, 'or a small one. I don't have time to deal with rats and mice. Rabbits are fun though.'

'What are rabbits?' Conker mewed.

'We can't stay long,' Soggy interrupted, 'I would very much like to, but we are on an ... important journey.'

Winter growled. 'The Red Wind rests, you will stay until she has heard our tales.'

'Of course,' Soggy dipped his head, 'Of course, for the tales, yes, but after that, when Arlyweh runs wild again, we must be on our way.'

Winter shuffled forward on her belly and stretched her muzzle to sniff Soggy's face, 'And how do you know so much about Red Wind, little cat?'

'I listened to a friend talk of her, just as he listened to me talk of Shadow White.'

Shadow White...? Conker remembered overhearing Gloworm mutter something about Shadow White when he was talking to Dust.

Winter pricked her tall fluffy ears, 'Who is your friend?'

'He runs with Red Wind now, but his name was, Skip, Faww Fraagoya.

Winter folded both her ears, tipped her head, and pricked one ear back up again. As the wind picked up, she closed her eyes and raised her muzzle. Conker watched her closely. Her ears moved like a cat's, tracking the sounds hiding in the wind. He let his own ears follow hers and detected a deep murmuring, right at the edge of his hearing. *There is something...*

When Winter opened her big brown eyes again, Conker saw that they were glimmering with sorrow. She nudged Soggy's cheek and woofed gently, 'Soggy Moggy gets my bed, but will never find my ball.'

All the fur along Soggy's spine stood on end and his tail bushed, but his scent did not fill with fear. *He's surprised...?* Conker watched closely as Soggy shifted his paws uneasily and flicked his ears as if suddenly surrounded. His good eye was wide and glistening with longing as he stared up at Winter.

'Soggy Moggy ... that's what the humans called me ... I always slept in Skip's bed. He hated it when I did that. And it wasn't his ball ... it was mine ... he stole it...' Soggy sniffed, then straightened, 'Did he say that? Did you hear him?'

Winter nodded, then shook her head, 'That's the last message he shared with the Ecewind. I don't hear him, just his words echoing forever.'

'How?' Conker shuffled closer to the dog, fascinated that she could hear so much in the wind, 'How can a voice echo forever? I have only ever known echoes to fade away.'

'In our Listenings,' Winter bowed her head to Conker, 'we listen to the messages in the wind. Then we repeat every word of every message that we hear. All dogs perform Listenings, so no message shared by any dog is ever lost. Our words do not die with us.'

'I remember Skip's Listenings,' Soggy sniffed, 'He was devoted to them. He'd stand for hours in the garden, barking every message he heard away into the wind. Then all the other dogs would hear his messages and join him, barking them onwards...' Soggy lifted is head and purred, 'I asked him once if he ever changed the messages. I even gave him the trial of changing the words... he didn't like that ... that's why he stole my ball.'

Winter let her tongue fall from her jaws as she panted, and there was a glint in her eye as she barked, 'And that is why the voices of cats fade away. Cats cannot follow rules.'

Soggy twitched his whiskers.

Conker recalled Briar trying to organise their first scout into the Long Box. *She's right... cats don't do well at following the rules...*

'And even now,' Winter went on, 'You demand I lay and tell my tale, and yet here we are, still lingering on small talk. You must know the rules well enough if you know how to command Red Wind. So, you must know that I will *ask* each of you for your tale, and after it is told, you will *ask* for mine.'

Soggy nodded, 'Of course, Winter, you may ask for my tale.'

Winter sniffed and licked her nose, 'Tell me the tale of what happened to your eye.'

'Nothing ... my eye is perfectly fine,' Soggy mumbled.

'The other one,' Winter sniffed.

Soggy nodded as he pulled the magic stick closer to him. Then after a long pause, he began his tale. 'I was going for a walk along a dark path. It was very dark and not a place a cat should ever walk alone, but The Warden of Trials will never, ever abandon a quest. So, I walked. Did I say I was alone? I was very alone...'

Winter nudged Soggy with her damp pink nose, 'If you want to get on your way, you should hurry your tale.'

'Yes, yes,' Soggy went on, 'I walked quickly, but not quick enough to escape their eyes. When they started to stare at me, I started to run, but I could not escape them ... It was *their* eyes that hurt my eye.'

Winter pricked her ears and tipped her head to one side, then woofed, 'The law of Red Wind says that you must tell your tale as honestly as you can. But there is no rule that says the listeners must believe you. Cats should stay away from dark paths. And their eyes are the only harmless things about them.'

Soggy shivered as he nodded, then he slumped down, pulled his stick close and sunk his teeth into it.

Winter looked at Conker, 'Now it's your turn. Tell me the tale of why you want to return to your prison.'

Conker closed his eyes and sighed, 'I want to get back to Fern.' he opened his eyes again and told Winter. 'She's still in The Boxes and she's afraid of everything. The humans treated her badly and I promised to protect her, and to hunt for her. She promised to always keep me company. But the first time I went hunting the Vast Tower Box, I chased a rat into a truck. I didn't know it was a truck, and before I could get out, it closed and trapped me inside. Then it brought me here. So, Soggy is helping me get back to her.'

'That is a good and honestly told tale,' Winter glanced at Soggy, 'Now, you may ask for a tale from me.'

Soggy sat up as tall as he could and mewed, 'Tell us the tale of who you are trying to find.'

Winter hung her head and whined. Then with a sorrowful sigh, she nodded, 'Very well.' She raised her head and began her tale. 'Nipper was the fastest dog I've ever known. I first met him shortly after I began my training. I was struggling to get a single sheep into its pen when my master called me to follow him up the hill, and there he was, in the valley below, effortlessly rounding up sheep into groups and driving them into their pens. We went up the hill to watch Nipper every day after that. I loved to watch him work, and not long after, we were allowed to work together. We became friends, and sometimes we would run off together after our work was done and explore the woods. We fell in love in those woods, we spoke of a life together... raising pups ... growing old with their pups... But it wasn't to be. Soon after that, my master stopped taking me to see him.

'I called to him every night, but he never answered. So, one day I escaped and ran to the valley to find him. He wasn't there. The farm cat told me he'd been taken away. I never saw him again, and I've never heard a single message from him in any of my Listenings. I lived my life wondering, every day, what happened to him. I've had mates of course, other dogs that I loved, and pups too, but I never loved any other dog as much as I'd loved Nipper. Maybe he forgot about me ... maybe he never loved me ... maybe he runs with Red Wind... I am too old to have pups now, so even if I did find him, we could never live the life we dreamt of, but I still have hope that maybe he has, at some time, tried to contact me ... and so I listen every day for his messages.'

Soggy sniffed and shuffled awkwardly, 'Have you tried climbing a tree?'

Winter shook her head. 'Why would I want to do that? That's a dumb thing cats do.'

'It's not as dumb as you might think.' Soggy purred, 'Cats climb trees for good reasons. It's amazing how much more you can see from the top of a tree.'

'And there you go again, little Soggy cat.' Winter let her tongue fall from her mouth as she panted with amusement, 'The rules of the Listenings imply quite clearly that you use your ears, not your eyes. Can any cat follow the rules?'

'But imagine how much further you could hear if you used your ears at the top of the tree, And I follow rules ... closely enough to discover ... where they can be broken. Perhaps the dutiful dogs could learn something from cat's ingenuity. Following rules ... is no guarantee of ... getting what you need.'

'Except balls?' Conker licked his shoulder, 'What is a ball anyway?'

Soggy twitched his whiskers, 'Balls are round things that bounce everywhere. They are hypnotic to dogs and quite useless for cats.'

Conker nodded. He remembered the humans throwing a round bouncing toy in The Old Place. He disagreed with Soggy, it had been great fun to chase.

Winter panted, then woofed, 'You've tickled my ribs, Soggy cat, I will try your tree idea, if you know of a tree that a dog could climb.'

'I do,' Soggy replied, 'not too far from here. At the end of this path before the long downward slope to the ... the...'

'Then let's go.' Winter thumped her tail on the floor and hopped to her paws. Then she watched, her head tipped to one side and her eyes glistening with amusement as Conker picked up the stick and crouched down to let Soggy clamber back up onto his back.'

9
Roads

The sun dragged the last of its light from the sky as they walked further down the path. Conker blinked as his eyes adjusted to the darkness, but it was like no darkness he'd ever experienced before. *What kind of darkness is still light...?* He slowed his pace and looked around, amazed at the silvery glow that had fallen over everything in The Outside.

Winter stopped and looked back at him, 'Are your paws too heavy with mud already?' she woofed, 'Or is Soggy slowing you down?'

Conker looked back over his shoulder. The little tom was snoring softly in his thick fur, and he felt warm. He still clutched his magic stick so tightly in his paws that it poked Conker in the ribs as he walked. 'He's not heavy, and the mud stuck to my paws is annoying, but it's not that...'

Winter snapped at something in the air, then tipped her head again, waiting for him to continue.

'It's the light,' Conker looked up into the sky.

'The Light?' Winter followed his gaze.

'Those tiny twinkling lights are all over it...'

'Stars,' Winter woofed.

'Stars?' Conker stared around at the countless little lights.

'Eyes ... of the ghosts...' Soggy mewed sleepily, 'prowling Ganlengan—'

'Balls.' Winter interrupted, 'Ghost balls, discarded by the dogs who run with Red Wind.'

'Eyes...'

'But they're not very bright,' Conker interrupted. 'Not bright enough to illuminate the entire of The Outside. Everything was so dark when the sun was in the sky, even though it was bright. But now it's gone, everything is even brighter.'

'Winter lolled her tongue and panted, then she flicked her nose to something behind him. 'The moon is up.'

'The ... what?' Conker looked behind him. In the sky, just above a line of trees hung a huge, bright silver crescent.

'The moon,' Winter repeated, 'a big glowing ball, great for chasing—'

'The Moon,' Soggy lifted his head a little, 'The eye of Uaelmyst, the Night Cat ... A slither as he prowls ... big and bright and round as he looks upon the world his daughter created.'

Conker twitched his whiskers and looked at Winter.

'Or a big ball,' she woofed, 'That you can chase to the end of the world.'

'It's not a ball now, it's a slither.'

'Because tonight, it hides behind the invisible ball.'

'You see, Conker,' Soggy mewed, 'no dog will ever understand the Night Cat's pride in Shadow White.'

'The Moon...' Conker sighed, as he looked up at the bright crescent beyond the trees. It seemed that cats and dogs had a different way of explaining The Outside. He tried to remember the main points of their explanations. 'It's bright, like an eye, or a ball.'

'And we should keep going, before the Night Cat returns to his mountain to sleep.'

'Before the ball bounces off the world and into the hands of the sun.'

'Or before we forget where we're going,' Conker purred as he began padding on again through the mud.

'Exactly,' Winter woofed as she turned and trotted off down the path. She splashed through the puddles as if they were fun, and every few paces she leapt up and snapped at the air.

'What are you trying to catch?' Conker asked, 'There's nothing there.'

'Night bugs!' Winter woofed as she leapt and snapped at the air again, 'look closely and you will see them flying around?'

Conker narrowed his eyes and watched the dog. After a while, he noticed a small whirling cloud of tiny glimmering dots near the hedge. Then another one hovering above a puddle. And suddenly, just like the stars, they were everywhere. Zipping and zooming about with movements that were faintly familiar. *They look like....* 'Flies?' Conker asked.

'And gnats, and moths, and midges and yes, lots of flies. All quite tasty if you want a snack.'

Conker nodded. He knew about flies. Sometimes they'd appeared in The Old Place and buzzed around uneaten food. *How did I not see them... What will my eyes and ears miss next....?* He stopped and shivered. Winter's playful bounding had kept his spirits high, but as more and more clouds of night bugs appeared, he began to feel anxious.

'Don't worry,' Soggy lifted his head and mewed, as if sensing his fear, 'We are quite safe ... while a dog travels with us ... they are the greatest protectors.'

Conker let out a deep breath. He trusted Soggy now. The little tom had been right about Winter, and he was sure he could trust her too. He watched her stop every few paces to sniff along the bottom of the hedge, or hesitate and sniff the air, her big fluffy ears pricked as she checked for danger in every shadow. He'd seen how ferocious she could be to anyone who wasn't a friend, but even with Soggy's reassurance, and Winter's protection, Dread pulled on his stomach as much as the mud sucked at his paws. Soggy felt easier to carry with every step, as if the warmer the little tom got, the lighter he became. *I need to find more food for him...* And there was something in the wind that made his fur prickle. Another sound, right on the edge of his hearing, familiar but menacing. Not like a voice that could be reasoned with.

'Are you coming?' Winter loped back to the cats, spraying them with more mud as she sploshed through another puddle.

'Yes,' Soggy mewed, 'Let's go.' He poked Conker in the ribs with his stick and wriggled back down into his thick fur.

Conker padded slowly after Winter.

'We go ... through the hedge,' Soggy mewed, 'This path goes down ... we need to go up. The tree you need is up the hill.'

'There's a hole a bit further along,' Winter barked.

Soggy lifted his head a whisker, 'The tree we are looking for has fallen ... so even a dog can climb into its topmost branches.'

'I'll go and look,' Winter barked excitedly as she spun around, bounded down the path, and disappeared through a hole in the hedge.

Conker trudged on after her, keeping his pace steady as Soggy rested his head and dug in his remaining little claws. He felt the path begin to slope just as the rain began to fall again. He gritted his teeth and let the water soak into his fur, unable to shake it off through fear of dropping Soggy. He was thankful for his warmth, but worried how the little tom would cope being soaked through from the rain.

The hole in the next hedge was a relief. Conker waited in the shelter of the sodden leaves and looked out across the grass to where a white blur gambolled about in the heavy rain. *How can she like this...?* he thought as his paws sank deeper into the mud.

At the sound of Winter's excited barking, Conker padded to the edge of the hole. She bounded towards him and slid to a halt in the mud, her tongue lolling merrily, 'I found it, come on, let's try this.'

'Soggy?' Conker turned to see the little tom slowly open his good eye, 'I'll try and be quick, so you don't get too wet. There's a lot of rain.'

'I quite ... enjoy the rain, it is good for keeping cool.'

Conker took a deep breath as Soggy gripped his stick tighter. *Likes the rain...? He told me no cat likes the rain... The wind must have blown all the fluff out of his ears... But he's getting hotter in my fur, so maybe the cold rain will be a relief...*

As Conker stepped out of the hedge, cold water ran over his paws. It was uncomfortable at first, but after a few steps, it began to soften the mud that clung to his fur, and he was thankful for the long, wet grass that brushed it away.

Winter raced back up the slope and sniffed around the raised roots of the fallen tree. Its trunk rested diagonally against the tree next to it, their branches tangled together. Conker followed the dog as quickly as he could, and by the time he'd reached the tree, she was already walking steadily up its trunk.

'You can let me down ... by the roots,' Soggy mewed, 'just there ... by that hole.'

Conker found the hole at the bottom of the trunk and held the stick while Soggy slid from his back. The little tom half walked, half dragged himself into the hollow tree and flopped down. Conker lay his stick by his side as Winter began to howl.

Once Soggy was settled, Conker hopped up onto the end of the tree trunk and ducked under a twisted knot of roots. Sheltered from the rain, he felt the wind rest to let Winter bark her message. When she was done, she cocked her head to the side and pricked her ears.

As he sat in companionable silence, Conker felt a low rumbling noise creep up through the fallen tree. He dug his claws into the soft flaky trunk and felt its vibration surge up through his legs. It was like the hum of The Boxes, a sound that rattles through you and everything around you. He could hear Winter breathing deeply as she awaited her reply. He could hear soggy snoring gently as he lay curled up with his magic stick in the hollow tree below. He could hear the wind in the trees and the rain as it pattered the earth around them. But he couldn't hear this sound, he could only feel it. He lifted his head and looked around for the source of the noise. He saw nothing, until the rain eased, and the dark clouds rolled away, and a bright orange light flickered into existence.

Winter lowered her head and whined. Soggy shifted and mumbled in his sleep. Conker glanced at the dog before he hopped down from the tree trunk and slid into the hollow tree. 'What's that noise. The one that I can feel?' he gently prodded Soggy with his paw.

The little tom felt limp, but he opened his good eye and lifted his head. 'Road...' he shivered.

'Road?' Conker could smell Soggy's fear scent as he leant closer, 'What's—'

'I found him!' The trunk bounced as Winter bounded excitedly back down it. She leapt from the low end and pushed her long white nose into the hole. 'I found him,' she woofed, 'I heard his message, he's on the other side of the mountains! Way up beyond the hills. You were right, Soggy Moggy, he *is* very high up.'

Soggy blinked at the dog, 'I'm glad ... you found him ... you should listen to cats ... more often,' he purred.

'I like listening to cats,' Winter woofed, 'and it's good to learn that you do talk sense sometimes. It has been good to travel with you both, but I must go. I need to get to the mountains before the sheep go to the high fields.' She sniffed Soggy's shoulder and tipped her head to Conker, 'I wish you good luck in your journey, take care of this little cat and keep him out of trouble.'

'I never ... get into trouble...' Soggy mewed, shuffling his legs around so he could push himself into a sitting position, 'The Warden of Trials is wise and—.'

Winter licked Soggy's face. He snorted and toppled backward, 'Look after him, Conker, and I hope you find Fern.'

'Thank you,' Conker dipped his head, 'I will take care of him.'

'Good to hear, and don't forget about my farm, there's always room for smart cats.'

Soggy sat himself up again and pulled his stick towards him. 'After we have found ... The Sign.'

'Then goodbye and good luck,' Winter sprang to her paws and turned a circle outside the hole, 'And stay away from the road,' she added before she bounded away through the rain.

The wind settled and the vibrating roar of the road intensified as Conker watched her go. When the last glimpse of her bright white fur had disappeared into the silvery night, he turned back to the little tom.

Soggy was shaking, his good eye wide with fear and his ears flicked around anxiously. 'Congratulations...' he mewed quietly, 'You have ... passed ... the First Trial.'

10
The Second Trial

Conker laid his tail over Soggy's back. The frail little cat was shivering, but not from the cold. As he felt the chilly wind whistle through the hollow fallen tree, Conker wondered how the little tom had stayed so warm.

A faint and distant howl cut through the wind. Winter was already far away, heading for the mountains to find her long lost love. Conker had felt safe in her company. She knew where to look for danger, constantly checking hedges and holes and puddles and shadows. Now it was up to him to look for threats, and that wasn't going to be easy in a place where he struggled to see what was right before his eyes. But he had to try. If anything happened to Soggy, he'd never see Fern again.

Darkness had woven its way through the trees and hedges as Conker slid out of the hollow trunk and looked around. There were more orange lights now. He stood on his hind legs and peered over the upended roots to look at them. As he watched them flicker, he felt the vibrating hum of the road work its way through the mud on his paws and creep up his legs.

With a painful wince, Soggy dragged himself and his stick out of the hollow trunk, and looked up at Conker, 'Are you ... ready for the Second Trial?'

Conker dropped back down to the ground, 'I think so.'

'You did well ... to carry me all this way.'

Conker crouched down next to the little tom and curled his thick fluffy tail around him. Soggy flopped down onto his belly and leant into Conker's side. 'Carrying you wasn't a problem,' he purred, 'It's the mud I don't like.'

Soggy purred, 'No cat likes mud. Mud is ... for dogs.'

'I could see that. I will miss Winter. She terrified me at first, but I can see she's a good friend to have.'

'Most dogs are the same. All defensive at first ... big teeth and bigger barks ... but most are good... Never forget how to command Red Wind ... it's a good trick to know.'

Conker nodded, 'I won't, but I doubt I'll meet any dogs in The Boxes.'

'Then let's get you back there ... let's start the Second Trial.'

Conker nodded, 'Okay.'

Soggy struggled to his paws and picked up his stick, then flicked an ear for Conker to follow. With his bent tail dragging uselessly in the mud, he limped around the roots of the hollow tree and through the sparse hedge behind it.

Conker let Soggy lean on him as they pushed through the hedge, but as they broke free of the tangled branches, the sight before them froze him to the spot. A meandering line of flickering orange lights cut the sky in half, and below them, a long dark path ran from one side of The Outside to the other. Conker couldn't see either end of it. On the path, two long rows of trucks raced headlong towards each other, glaring at each other with their bright glowing eyes. The low rumbling growl travelled further up his legs, through his body, and out into his ears, just as a familiar acrid stench stung his nose. As he watched, he noticed with amazement that the trucks never collided, despite their speed and aggression. They slid effortlessly past each other before racing onwards and vanishing into the distance. He felt dizzy as he tried to follow them with his eyes, but he couldn't tear his gaze away from their mesmerising motion.

Soggy shivered as he leant into Conker's shoulder, took a deep breath and with a solemn voice, he mewed,

*'A path deadly dark,
'To cross it you face your light,
'And try you will fail.'*

Conker listened carefully to Soggy's words. He tried to think the riddle through, but the noise and stench of the trucks at the bottom of the hill tugged at his mind. He could feel Soggy trembling beside him, and his fear scent was almost as strong as their acrid stench. The more he watched, the more impossible it became to see how they could avoid crashing into each other. He locked his eyes onto one and tried to follow it, but it was too fast. He tried again, following it further this time. On his third attempt, he managed to follow it as it raced away into the undulating hills in the distance, all the time following the same dark path. *A path deadly dark... A road...?* Conker turned to soggy, 'You want me to cross that?'

Soggy dropped his stick and nodded slowly.

'Face your light?' Conker asked, 'you mean I have to face their lights to cross it?'

Soggy shook his head, 'There is a light ... that we all face at the end of our lives. A good light ... the soft white glow of Shadow White. When you cross a road ... it is not the light of the trucks that you really face... The light ... you face ... is hers...'

Conker's skin prickled. *At the end of our lives...? ... Are we going to die...?* He was beginning to get an idea of who Shadow White might be. 'And I will fail?' he mewed, 'Fail to what?'

'To cross it.'

'But you want me to cross it?'

'To reach The Sign ... you must cross the road. But it ... cannot ... be crossed. And even if you try ... if those wheels hit you ... you will die ... and Shadow White will not ... be able to ... unflatten you enough to ... let you ... return.'

I die...? Conker hung his head and took a deep breath. *Wheels...?* 'What are wheels?'

'Their round black feet...'

Conker recalled hiding behind the round black foot of the truck he'd escaped from. It had been big enough to conceal him in its shadow, and there had been barely enough room for him to stand behind it. The trucks on the road moved so fast, he doubted that he'd be able to avoid their wheels. But if it was the only way to The Sign, he had to cross the road. He had to get back to Fern.

Soggy slumped down onto the damp earth and pulled his stick towards him. As he bit down hard onto it, his whole body shuddered with fear and heat.

Conker took a deep breath. *Maybe it is impossible for a cat like Soggy, a cat who could barely stand up straight, let alone walk. But, for me...? It will be dangerous... I will have to cross quickly after one truck has passed... and before the next one comes along... I can do this...* He watched them again, racing towards each other. They never hit each other because they left plenty of space around them. He narrowed his eyes and peered closer. There was a faint white line down the middle of the road. It separated the two rows and kept them on their own side. If he was quick enough, he could get through one row of trucks, then wait on the line for a gap in the next. He was just about to tell Soggy his idea when one of the trucks in the nearest row slowed, flashed an orange light, swung over the white line and through a gap in the trees. Conker gasped. *What if we'd been waiting on that line...?*

'They never ... stop ... They never ... sleep ... Nothing ... can stop them...' Soggy panted, as if reading Conker's thoughts.

'Never?'

'They race ... towards each other ... like mates, but they never ... meet each other. But... they will meet ... anything ... that stands in their path...'

Conker looked further along the road. In the distance he could make out the bright white lights as the trucks sped towards them, and the dimmer red lights as they raced away. A flashing orange light appeared on another truck, just before it turned away from the others. Conker watched as it slowed and then stopped. Then its lights went out. *They do stop...*

'They will take us all ... to Shadow White,' Soggy mewed.

There must be a way... But the longer Conker stood watching, the clearer it became that Soggy was right, the trucks never stopped on the road. They only stopped after they'd left it.

'There is ... no way to cross ... they never stop ... we can't fly over it ... it goes on forever ... we cannot go around it ... we can't dig under it...' Soggy's fear scent was overpowering, his voice was trembling. He bit down harder on his stick and growled.

Conker looked up at the sky. Tiny black shapes swooped and soared in the billowing clouds above the road, gliding from the trees on one side to the trees on the other. *Birds...*

'We cannot cross it ... we will never cross it...'

'We can't go over it,' Conker mewed, 'But the birds can. They can fly. But we can dig, so, we must be able to dig under it.'

Soggy hissed. The magic stick crunched between his teeth.

Conker scanned the edge of the road, looking for somewhere to dig a hole, and was amazed when he spotted a dark round circle in the grassy slope below it, half hidden by a bush. 'There!' he leapt to his paws, 'Look, Soggy, there's already a hole under it.'

Soggy dropped his stick. 'We cannot go under it ... we cannot go under it...' his good eye went wide as he shuffled back into the hedge.

'Why not?' Conker mewed, 'That is a hole, isn't it?'

'Hole ... yes,' Soggy growled.

'Does it go all the way under the road?'

Soggy sighed, 'Yes.'

Conker swished his tail. He looked down at Soggy, 'If we can't cross it, or go round it, or fly over it, then why can't we go under it through that hole?'

'Cats cannot use that hole. It's their hole...'

'Whose hole...'

'The ... rats...'

Conker purred and gave Soggy's ear a lick. 'Did you say rats?'

'Yes ... a deadly gang ... of rats ... guard that hole ... I have heard of cats crossing roads without ... meeting Shadow White, but cats ... cannot get through rat holes.'

'Then it's time this deadly gang of rats met a Ratter.'

'A Ratter!' Soggy gazed up at Conker, 'Of course ... you are...' He flopped his head down onto his stick and sighed with relief. Then his eye widened again, and he looked back up at Conker, 'But ... they are ... no ordinary rats... They are Ards.'

Conker twitched his whiskers. He'd not met enough rats to know what that meant, but the one he'd chased with the white rump was no ordinary rat either. He nudged Soggy gently, 'Don't worry, I know how to deal with rats,' he hoped that was true, 'The last time my friends and I met a group of rats, rats died, and cats did not.'

'You are a Ratter, Conker. You are big ... and strong and brave. And I am the Warden of Trials ... I am smart and wise, and a keeper of secret knowledge. But I am small, and ... weak. You must do this alone. You will get past these rats... I am certain. You will outrun them... and you will out fight them. But if I go with you... they will pull me from your back ... and send me to Shadow White in more pieces than she'd know what to do with... No cat has ever walked through a rat hole.'

Conker raised his chin and ruffled his fur. 'Then it's about time some cat did.'

11
Ratters

Conker slowed his pace as he approached the dark and ominous hole. The circle of slimy square stones around its edge glistened in the rain. The hole was large enough for him to walk through with Soggy on his back, but the bit of floor he could see was uneven and strewn with debris. The strong stench of decay and rats overpowered the already harsh smell of the trucks that raced along the road above.

As he took a step forward and reached out a paw to the slimy stones, Conker remembered walking down the Long Box under the dull yellowish glow of the roof lights, and into the gloomy Dark Corner. He put his paw down on the stone and peered into the same menacing darkness, widening his eyes as he searched for the first sign of movement. Everything moved around the hole, the grass, the scudding clouds above him, the falling raindrops, but the darkness within the hole remained still. He edged closer. His fur rising with every breath, until fresh rat scent rolled across his tongue, and squealing voices met his ears.

'Cat. Back. Back.'

'Cat!'

'Stop. Cat.'

Conker froze. He trained his ears on the muffled voices, *Two... Three... More....?* He couldn't make out how many voices there were. *Can I fight three rats....?* The image of Spinney slumped against the wall in the Long Box flashed across his mind. Two rats had attacked Spinney... He took a step back. *No...* He stopped again. *No... I must face them...*

'Were cat?' a small grating voice peeped.

'Out pipe.'

'Out.'

What did Gloworm say...? What was that rat's name...?

'I scare cat. Back. Back,' came the grating voice again.

Conker heard claws scraping on stone, then a moment later, faint shuffling paw steps and a skittish shadow edged closer to the entrance. *Steel...? No... Skeeal...!*

'Cat. Shoo. Away.'

Conker took a deep breath. *This is the only way to cross the Road... The only way to find The Sign... the only way back to Fern...* 'Skeeal? he mewed, 'Is that you? I have come from The Boxes.'

'Skeeal!'

Claws scraped frantically on stone and splashed through unseen water. Conker leant closer and flicked his ears. *They're scared....?*

'Cat say Skeeal?'

Conker stepped forward. *Are they afraid of Skeel....?*

'Cat no come pipe.'

As the shadows shifted again, Conker leant a little closer.

'Cat. Stop.'

Are they scared of me too....? He took one more careful step forward and mewed kindly into the darkness, 'Hello rats. I don't want to come into your pipe, I just want to find Skeeal.'

'Skeeal gone. Cat got message?'

'A message?' Conker purred, 'of course, I have a message for Skeel.'

'What message?'

'An important one. So Skeeal should be the first to hear it,'

'Hear what?'

Conker sighed, 'The message.'

'What cat name?'

'Conker.'

'Ard-er Braew. Cat no move. Ard-er Braew see cat.' A pointy whiskered nose slid out of the hole, followed by a sleek brown head with small beady eyes. The rat's whiskers twitched, and its eyes widened as they looked up Conker's legs, up his shoulders, and up to his face. Then with a squeal, the eyes vanished back into the darkness, 'Cat. Big!'

Conker lifted his head and sat up as tall as he could and listened to the rats scrabbling and squealing inside the pipe. *They are afraid...* He waited until they fell silent and the faint paw steps came back to the edge of the stones.

'Why cat big?'

'Because I'm a Ratter.'

'What Rat-er?'

'A big cat. Bigger than all cats in The Outside, that's what a ... friend of mine told me.'

'Soggy cat?'

'Er... yes ... Soggy.'

'Bad cat!'

'No!' Conker felt his fur rise, 'He's not a bad cat, he's just a bit strange. Okay, he's the strangest cat I've ever met ... and I know Gloworm—'

'Where Rat-er from?'

Conker shook himself and went on, 'I'm from The Boxes. My friends and I were taken there by the humans to kill the rats. We are all big, the same size as me. They are still there but I escaped in a truck and came here.'

'Escape? Bring message? What message?'

'Well,' his shoulders sagged. *Message...?* He couldn't think of anything to say, 'I don't know...'

'Cat not know?'

Conker hung his head, 'I have no idea. I just came here.' He leant forward and flicked his ears. He could hear the other rats milling about a good leap away from their leader. He parted his jaws, letting their scent flow over his tongue. If he was quick, he could dive into the darkness and grab this rat. *Maybe without their leader...*

'YOU MESSAGE!'

'What?' Conker jumped.

'Make sense!'

Scratching and squeaking echoed from the depths of the gloom as the hidden rats shuffled closer again.

'What makes sense?' Conker mewed?

'Big cat. That *is* message.'

Just a little closer... Conker stretched out a paw and put it down softly on the nearest stone. Twitching whiskers caught the dull moonlight and gleamed in the darkness. He reached out his nose and parted his jaws, ready to lunge in and take the rat with one bite. But before he could shuffle his hind legs into position, Ard-er Braew darted out of the pipe and dove into a clump of tall grass on the other side of the hole.

'Tell Ard-er Braew about Rat-er,' he squeaked as he poked his head up from the tall grass, 'What for? Where come from?'

The rat was out of reach now. Conker flicked his ears to the rats still in the pipe. They were slinking closer. If he was to catch their leader, he would have to move across the entrance, and if he did that, the rats skulking in the shadows would attack him. He sighed and sat down. *They knew what I was trying to do...* He decided to talk while he thought of a new plan. 'I come from The Boxes, but before that I lived in The Old Place. That's where I was born, with my brother Acorn and sister, Petal. They were big too. Acorn was bigger than me...' Conker hung his head for a moment and wondered where his siblings were now. *Still in The Old Place...? In other Boxes...? They'll be fine. I'm the one in The Outside, the one in trouble...*

'How bigger?'

Conker shook his thoughts away, 'Acorn is taller than me and his paws are bigger.'

'Why so big?' Ard-er Braew bent the grass down with a paw as he lent forward to peer at Conker, 'What made cat big?'

'The humans, I think. They came to give us milk and they cleaned us. Some of the other Ratters had mothers to do that, but we didn't ... not that I remember. It was the humans that raised us.'

'Why human make cat big?

'I don't know. I don't know why they do anything. They made us hunt Ratbots in The Old Place and if we caught them, we won our food. But when I went to The Boxes with the other Ratters, there were no Ratbots, just rats, and thats when we understood that rats were food and we had to kill them all ourselves.'

'All?' Ard-er Braew flinched, and then he shrieked, 'PROMISE!'

Conker jumped to his paws. Claws scuffled in the shadows. There was something in Ard-er Braew's voice that made his fur ripple along his spine. 'Promise ... what? He mewed.

'The Promise ... human make big cat. Kill all rat. Cat break deal.'

'Deal?' Conker twitched his whiskers, 'What deal?'

'This bad. Bad for rat. Bad for cat. Bad. Bad!'

Conker sat down again and sighed. He wasn't sure if he was getting anywhere. 'I don't know what you mean, I just came here to find—'

'Skeeal? Skeeal bad rat. Better cat food. Skeeal not here.' Ard-er Braew slid out of the grass and looked at Conker. 'Conker good cat. Trust Conker.'

Conker dipped his head, 'Well, thank you, I er...'

'Conker take pipe. Ard-er Braew go. Warn Rat King.'

Panicked squeaks and squeals came from the darkness. Conker held his breath and watched wide eyed as Ard-er Braew waved his tail and beckoned the rats out of the pipe. Hundreds of them. He felt his skin tingle as they slid past him and congregated around their leader. *Good job I didn't attack...*

'Good Conker,' Ard-er Braew peeped when all the rats were safely behind him. 'Trust Conker. Good Cat. Go in now. Keep pipe safe. Look in Clooie for gift.'

'Gift?' Conker glanced at the pipe, Clooie?'

Ard-er Braew bowed to Conker, 'Down, Clooie down, where rat from. Gift to good cat in Clooie.'

Conker dipped his head and watched as the lead rat turned and slithered away into the shadows. The others followed, their only sound the silky rustle of their fur against the long grass. When they had gone and the grass had stilled, Conker peered into the dark pipe, *A gift...? From rats...?* He took a deep breath. *How bad can it be...?*

The roar of the trucks on the road above slowly filled the silence. He'd blocked out the noise to focus on the subtle sounds of the rats, but he could hear everything again now, the chirping of the birds, the rustling and creaking of the trees, the swishing of the grass ... the faint whimpering squeaks of a rat... Conker flicked his ears. *There's one left...*

One rat can't hurt a Ratter... Conker stood up and stepped into the darkness. He sniffed the air but couldn't separate the stench of rat and rot. He listened again. The squeaking was faint and pitiful. He took another step, gasping as he felt the sharp coldness of water under his paws. Once inside the pipe he stopped to let his eyes adjust to the darkness and was relieved to discover that it wasn't as dark as it had appeared from outside.

The pipe was long, but he could see a faint greyish light at the other end. The square stones lined the entire of the circular walls and roof. The floor was flatter, but still rounded enough to collect puddles, and it was strewn with broken objects, some human and some the twisted remains of trees and hedges. In the middle of the floor, about halfway along the pipe, there was a perfectly round patch, dark enough to be a hole. The distressed squeaking was coming from inside it. *The Clooie...?*

Conker padded closer. The scent of rat from the hole strengthened, and when he stopped by the slippery stones at its edge, it overpowered every other smell. Even the rot and the stench of the road that echoed above. Even his own fear scent. He peered into the hole. It was wide enough to be one good leap across, and deep enough for a jump down into it to need some thought. The dim light in the pipe was just enough to illuminate half of the waterlogged floor and the pile of debris at the bottom of the hole. The other side of the hole was cast in shadow. Conker couldn't be sure what lurked there, but whatever it was rippled the surface of the water.

A rat's tail flicked out of the shadow, shivered, and slid back in. *Just one rat...?* Conker leant into the hole and sniffed. There was so much rat stench that he couldn't be sure if it *was* just one. He hesitated, wondering if it was a trap, but the squeaking came again, pained, and laboured. *It's hurt...*

Conker focused on a dry patch of floor between the puddles and dropped his shoulders. If he kept his tail up, he could land there easily and keep it, and his paws, out of the water. He leant forward, padded his paws down the inside wall and pushed off. He landed neatly but jumped back into the pile of debris as the rat's tail flicked out again and brushed his leg.

'Rat ... gone...?' squeaked a shaky little voice.

Conker straightened himself and flicked the water from his paws. Slowly, he edged towards the voice in the shadows and mewed, 'Yes. They went to warn the Rat King.'

'Ard-er Braew ... leave ... Gioot.'

'Gioot?' Conker padded into the shadows. A single rat lay crumpled on the floor, her head pressed against the wall, and her hind legs bent at impossible angles behind her. She was breathing rapidly, her mouth open, and her tongue lolled to one side. 'What happened to you?' Conker asked.

'Stone fall ... crush legs. Gioot hurt. Who cat?'

'I'm Conker,' he edged closer and sniffed the rat. Her scent was fresh, but he could smell the blood on her fur. His stomach rumbled. *Gift...* He pulled his head away as he remembered the boss rat's words, and mewed kindly, 'Is this your Clooie? Ard-er Braew told me to Look in the Clooie for a gift.'

'Clooie down ... Gioot gift.'

'What?' Conker mewed.

'Gioot legs broke ... dead soon. Gioot gift ... for good cat.'

'I don't understand,' Conker tipped his head to one side, 'how are you a gift?'

'Gioot ... dead ... gift now ... food gift ... for cat.'

Conker watched as she tipped her head back and curled her tail over her broken legs. Then he leant in and sniffed her neck. His mouth began to water as he bit gently into her soft fur.

'Gioot ... thank ... Conker.'

Conker took a deep breath and sunk his teeth into the soft flesh on Gioot's neck. He closed his eyes and waited as her warm blood flowed over his tongue. Waited until her breathing had ceased. Waited until she fell limp. 'Thank you, Gioot,' he mumbled as he lifted her body from the waterlogged floor. He needed to eat. Soggy needed to eat.

12
The Glaring of Ghosts

Conker dropped the dead rat beside the fallen tree. 'Soggy,' he mewed quietly, 'the rats have gone, the tunnel is clear.' He pushed his head into the hole and felt the stuffy warmth that filled the trunk. The little tom was curled up in a dip in the floor, his ears flicked once before he slowly raised his head.

Soggy shook away some bits of crumbling tree and turned to Conker, 'Clear? You killed ... all the rats?'

'I didn't need to,' Conker purred, 'They left. They went to warn the Rat King.'

Soggy blinked his good eye in surprise, 'They ... left? Rat King?'

'Yes. Their leader got scared because I'm big, and he said something about a promise, and a deal. Then they all left and asked me to look after the pipe. Except this one,' he nudged the dead rat, 'they left her as a gift. She was injured.'

Soggy tipped his head to one side, nodded slowly, and mumbled, 'A gift ... yes. The deal ... of course. A Ratter ... big cats ... that would be a worry for them.' He lifted his head as high as it would go and stared at Conker, 'Well, I never! And the tunnel, their pipe ... is it safe?'

'Safe enough.'

Soggy sighed with relief as he shakily lifted himself to his paws. 'Then we eat ... and then we go ... The Third Trial isn't far away.' He lent down, picked up his stick, and dragged himself uncomfortably out of the trunk.

'Good idea,' Conker agreed, and as Soggy settled down beside him, he began tearing small pieces of flesh from the dead rat.

Soggy dropped his stick and took the first piece. He chewed slowly at first, but after a few heartbeats, he found his appetite. Conker let the little tom eat his fill and finished off the generous remains. They didn't fill his belly, but he could hunt again later.

After they'd finished eating, Conker helped Soggy climb back onto his back, and was surprised at the amount of heat flowing from his frail body. *How can he be so hot...?* He set off at a steady walk, but as soon as they were heading downhill, Soggy began to slip. Conker turned his head and grabbed the little tom's scruff to steady him. 'Hold on tight,' he mewed, 'the pipe is dark, and its floor is wet and uneven, I don't want you to fall off.'

Soggy purred and gripped a little tighter with the few claws he had. Once he was secure again, Conker set off carefully down the hill towards the pipe. Soggy tensed as they neared the road. The acrid stench of the trucks wafted around them as they growled and screeched past each other in their endless race into the distance. Conker welcomed the overpowering smell of rats when they reached the silent pipe.

As they entered the pipe, Soggy lifted his head and groaned, 'Are you sure ... the rats ... have gone?'

Conker stopped and listened. He could hear the rumbling of the trucks, and a slow dripping of water, but the scratching and squeaking sounds had left with the rats. As the cold air crept through the pipe, Conker let it glide over his tongue. The scent of rat was growing stale, but he couldn't be sure there weren't more lurking in their Clooie. He took a deep breath, 'Yes,' he told Soggy, 'Im sure we are safe.'

'I hope so. A fight with rats ... will be ... the end of me.'

Conker felt his stomach tighten. *Please be gone...* It would only take one remaining rat, lurking in wait somewhere, to start a fight. *Can I fight with a cat on my back...?* He shook the thoughts away, 'Don't' worry, the other side is not far, we will be through in no time. Just hold on tight.'

Soggy rested his head back down and mewed, 'As tight as I can.'

As Conker walked on through the water and the debris, he kept his eyes and ears fixed on the dull light at the end of the pipe, and his ears on the hole in the middle, listening for the slightest scratch or sniff of a remaining rat. But the Clooie remained silent.

As he stepped into the dull light, Conker slowed his pace. Dread gnawed at his stomach. They should be on the other side of the road, but he could no longer hear the trucks. An eerie silence filled his ears as he let his eyes follow the ominous shadows that skittered across the slimy square stones. 'What's out there?' he mewed.

'The ... lane,' Soggy mewed quietly, 'The lane ... to the Third Trial.'

Conker peered out into the narrow lane. It was closed in on both sides by tall dense hedges and overcast by a canopy of sparse trees. The silvery light of the moon dripped through their branches and dappled the glimmering floor, illuminating brightly coloured slicks that slid over the surface of slimy puddles and around muck crusted stones. Ripe frowsty scents clung to everything, overpowering even the lingering stench of the trucks. It was as if the wind refused to come here to clean the air.

Soggy dropped his stick.

Conker watched as the stick rolled off the square stones, fell onto the glimmering floor, and began to sink. *It's mud... rotten mud...*

'My ... stick...'

'I'll get it.'

'Carry it ... for me...'

'Okay, hold on tight,' Conker bent down carefully and pulled the stick from the mud, gripped it tightly in his jaws and when he felt Soggy dig in his claws again, he stepped forward onto the gloomy Lane. His paws sunk slowly as the glimmering mud oozed up between his toes. The deathly cold air made him shiver and for once he was thankful for the heat radiating from the little tom's body.

Every time he lifted a paw, the mud clung to it and sucked it back down. But Conker kept going, biting down hard on the Magic stick as Soggy slept fitfully in the fur on his back. The dappled light cast on the floor by the branches above quivered as his paws displaced the colours in the mud. All around them, the long, dank grasses that sprouted from the mud and the tangled hedges hung their heads hopelessly.

Shadows encroached every corner of his vision and as the clouds rolled in the moonlight, one of the shadows shifted. He stopped. His fur began to rise. Something was hiding in the grass.

Conker barely noticed his paws sinking deeper into the mud as he stared at the long, twisted shapes in the shadowy grass. He flicked an ear back to Soggy. When the little tom didn't stir, he heaved a paw out of the mud and took a step towards the grass, stretching out his neck and parting his jaws. The scents were the same. Whatever it was had no scent of its own. He took another step forward, then another until he could make out something coiled in loops through the grass. It reminded him of a huge rat tail, but it didn't smell of rat. When it didn't move, he reached out a muddy paw and nudged one of the coils. It rocked slightly and slumped to the ground. *Human thing...* Conker sighed. He'd seen something like it before but much smaller and thinner. The humans had used it to entice him to chase. *String ... giant string...*

Feeling relieved, Conker backed out of the grass and looked around. But as his eyes fell on other strange shapes in the wilting grass, his skin began to prickle. *There are human things ... everywhere...* He trudged through the mud to the other side of the lane. Everywhere he looked he could see strange, yet familiar objects tangled in the grass. Smashed and strewn bowls of all different sizes dotted the ground. Torn pieces of shiny covers hung from the decaying twisted branches of the hedge. Fragments of full boxes clung to the edge of the muddy path. Conker bit down on the stick as he took it all in. *What did this....?*

With his ears pricked and alert for any new sound, Conker padded on along the gloomy lane. *There's nothing to fear...* His fur rippled as his eyes scanned the broken human things and the eerie shadows in the deathly silence. He hadn't gone much further when the sharp scent of metal traps, like cold blood, filled his nose.

Conker stopped again. Soggy took a deep rattling breath and shivered. The heat from his frail body was the only thing that felt comfortable on the forlorn lane. 'What is this place?' he mewed.

'Keep ... walking ... it ... is ... safe...'

Conker lifted his chin and took a deep breath, trying to avoid the fetid stench that seeped from the mud as his paws sunk deeper. He didn't feel safe, but he trusted Soggy. He didn't know what kind of creature had destroyed the human things around him, but he forced his fur to flatten and took another small breath. *If it's safe for soggy, it's safe for me...* There was a corner just ahead, the path around it marked out buy a long heap of bulging shiny covers.

Conker padded on past the stinking heap and followed the muddy path around the corner. The further he went, the more broken human things he could see. His eyes were so busy trying to make sense of all the complicated shapes that he didn't see the tall dark figure stood in the middle of the lane until he almost walked into it. He caught his breath and froze.

'He ... is ... safe...' Soggy mewed.

Conker sniffed the figure. *Dog...* He took a step back. The dog stood facing down the lane on tall, crooked legs. Far taller than Winter. Conker lowered his eyes. After a few heartbeats, the dog sniffed, and began walking away.

'Follow ... him.'

As Conker began padding after the huge grey bristly furred dog, he noticed it was carrying something in its jaws. Something floppy, like a bundle of covers. Conker bit down harder on Soggy's magic stick.

'Safe ... follow...'

The dog trudged slowly down the lane. Its huge hairy paws gouging gullies in the mud that quickly refilled with colourful greasy water. Its tail drooped, and its head hung low with the weight of the bundle that swayed with every slow nod of its head. Soggy twitched and shifted in Conker's fur and loosened his grip.

Conker dropped the stick. 'Soggy, hold on,' he mewed, 'I don't want you to fall off into this.'

The dog flicked a floppy ear but kept on walking.

Soggy dug his claws in again.

Conker picked up the stick and padded on after the dog. It was heading towards a huge hedge at the end of the lane, but it wasn't like any hedge Conker had ever seen before. Rather than the softly twisting tangle of branches of the hedges on either side of them, this one was constructed in harsh symmetrical lines and uniform corners, bent at straight yet frightful angles. He kept his eyes on the strange hedge as they walked closer, searching for a hole or other way of getting through. It was nothing like the thorny tunnels they'd passed through before, yet there was something frustratingly familiar about it. He closed his eyes and shook his head. When he opened his eyes again, he recognised the shapes. *trucks...?* The hedge before him was made from piles of twisted and broken trucks.

The dog stepped out of the mud, padded through the wilted grass and up a small slope. He stopped in front of the truck hedge and dropped the bundle. It hit the ground with a dull thud. The dog peered down at it for a few heartbeats, then he lifted his head and woofed quietly, 'I am sorry.'

'Stay ... still...' Soggy mewed.

Trust Soggy... He dropped his gaze, keeping his eyes just high enough to see what was happening, but he couldn't see the bundle clearly behind the dog's huge hairy paws.

A shadow shifted in the truck hedge. Conker raised his eyes and followed it as it slipped out of the broken trucks and slid into the drooping grass at the side of the lane. The shadow emerged from the grass again in front of the huge dog. Then two bright yellow eyes opened, and the gravelly voice of an old grey she-cat meowed, 'Thank you, Wellington.'

'Cats.' Conker mewed with relief.

'Yes,' replied Soggy.

Wellington nodded to the she-cat and turned around. Conker tensed as the huge dog padded towards him, but Wellington only paused to dip his head politely as he passed, before sloshing away along the lane.

When the big dog had padded around the corner and out of sight, Conker looked back at the she-cat. She had been joined by a large ginger tom and a small white tom. All three were staring at the bundle on the floor. Conker followed their gaze and gasped as his eyes fell on the crumpled body of a cat. The magic stick fell from his jaws.

Soggy dug a claw into his ribs.

When Conker looked up again, the she-cat was staring at him. She flicked her tail and mewed, 'Welcome friends, to the Glaring of Ghosts.'

13
Shadow Song

Conker took a step forward, 'I—'

'Hush!' the she-cat hissed, 'The time for you to speak will come. First, we attend to our departed friend.'

Soggy purred as Conker stepped back and dipped his head.

The old she-cat slowly got to her paws and gazed up into the sparse branches above. Her eyes darted about for a moment, as if searching for something. Then she threw back her head and yowled, '*SHARA GANS EVY...*'

Conker twitched his whiskers. He'd never heard any cat speak this language.

The she-cat yowled again, '*GWERES EVY KLEWES...*'

Something shifted in the hedge. As Conker turned to look, a fluttering sound came from the other side of the lane.

'*AGAS KOV...*'

Soggy lifted his head.

Conker flicked his ears, trying to lock them onto the rustling and flapping sounds that seemed to come from everywhere.

DRI EV OMMA...'

The tom cats padded to the she-cat's side, and as she lifted her chin and yowled again, they joined in.

'KAVOS Y HANOW...
'PIW EIS EV...
'DIWEDH Y PAYN...
'GASA EV RYDH...'

The rustling and fluttering intensified in the hedges. Conker stepped back, but Soggy dug in a claw, 'Stay ... still.'

The toms closed their eyes and lowered their heads, and the she-cat yowled alone again,

'SHARA GANS EVY...
'GWERES EVY KLEWES...
'AGAS KOV...
'DRI EV OMMA...'

On her last word, hundreds of birds launched themselves up and out of the hedges and trees around them. They rose as one spiralling murmuration across the dark gloomy sky with a deafening cacophony of flapping and chattering and chirping and fluttering.

Soggy purred and rested his head.

Conker held his breath as he watched the birds swirl and spread and vanish into the distant clouds. When he could see them no more, he looked down at the grey she-cat. He could see her old bones moving stiffly under her silvery grey coat. White flecks of fur framed her sleek narrow face and drew out her sunken yellow eyes. She dipped her head, then padded towards him with an air of authority that negated her frailty.

'Thank you for your patience,' she mewed kindly as she sat down stiffly in front of Conker, I am Meo'keo, Orar'rai, Mik'emer Piar, Misty,' she tipped her head and looked Conker up and down, 'You may call me Misty. Now, you were saying?'

Conker dipped his head, 'I am Conker and the cat I'm carrying is Soggy—'

'Soggy?' the large ginger tom leapt to his paws. The small white tom shuffled uneasily.

'What happened to him?' Misty narrowed her eyes as she moved to Conker's side and sniffed the little tom's foreleg.

Soggy lifted his head, 'I am ... fine. I am ... helping ... Conker...'

'Fine you are not,' Misty hissed as she padded back to the path and flicked her tail to Conker, 'bring him into the den.'

Conker followed Misty along a narrow muddy track that led through an upside-down truck. He kept his ears on her soft paw steps and his head low to watch his own. Rotting brambles snaked around the twisted metal and obscured the puddles of stagnant water that had collected beneath them, but despite their pungent stench, he still struggled to avoid them.

'Follow me, step where I do.' The ginger tom mewed as he padded ahead of Conker and lifted a lifeless bramble with his nose. 'I'm Mara'rua Wisa, Mellow, and this is Kii'iska Awak, Crispy.'

Conker nodded to Mellow. He was bigger than the other outdoor cats, but still smaller than himself. Crispy wasn't much bigger than Soggy, but he looked plumper, younger, and healthier than Misty and Soggy.

As they neared the other side of the upside-down truck, Misty reached up and pulled a thorny tendril away from a jagged hole, 'You will need to bend your knees here, the hole is small,' she blinked at Conker, then slipped through. Mellow nudged Crispy to the other side of the hole and together they held the tendril back for Conker to go through.

Conker dropped into a crouch and crawled forward on his belly. He didn't want to risk bumping Soggy on the twisted jagged metal above them. He could barely feel the little tom's breathing. His body heat was the only reminder that he was still there.

As he emerged from the hole, Conker lifted his head and looked around the den. It was a small clearing, barely three good leaps from end to end, and enclosed by piles of twisted and broken trucks that were overshadowed by gangly tree branches. Above the branches, he could see the thick grey clouds scudding across the sky in the soft eerie glow of the moon. Thick patches of intertwined brambles and long grasses grew around the edge of the den, some reaching far into the centre, while others clung to the twisted metal around the edge. Conker could see holes and flat patches within them that looked like good places to sleep. In the centre of the den, the floor raised into a mound of dry earth, and on top of the mound lay the black round foot of a truck *A Wheel...?*

Misty trudged across the clearing, hauled herself onto the wheel and flicked her tail twice. 'Mellow, Crispy, bring our departed friend inside while we wait.' Then she looked at Conker, 'And you, bring Soggy to me.'

As the two toms headed back to the lane, Conker straightened himself up and padded to Misty. He crouched down again to let the Soggy, but he didn't move.

Misty climbed back down from the wheel and tapped Soggy's head with her paw, 'Wake up,' she meowed.

Soggy lifted his head and groaned, 'Misty?'

'Yes. You are back with the Glaring of Ghosts. Now get off this huge friend of yours and tell me what you have been doing.'

Soggy purred and began to slide from Conker's back. Misty grabbed his scruff to steady him to the floor and began sniffing him over. Conker waited quietly until Mellow and Crispy dragged the body of the dead cat through the hole and laid it carefully beside the wheel.

Conker stared down at the cold crumpled body of the dead cat. It was a young tom, who's tabby coat with white belly and paws had been healthy and well-groomed before mud and blood had stained it. His eyes were closed, and his tongue lolled lifelessly. He glanced at Soggy. Apart from the colour of their fur, he could see little other difference between them. Conker's stomach sank, and his breath felt heavy. *How did he get like this....?*

'What happened to him?' Mellow padded to Misty's side and sniffed Soggy's flank. It rose a little, then dropped again.

'Will he die as well?' Crispy crouched down beside Mellow, his eyes wide with shock.

Conker glanced at the dead cat.

'Not yet.' Misty sat up and stared at Conker, 'What happened to him?'

Conker shook his head, 'I don't know, he said he only needs one eye to see, and tails lie and that he didn't want to use all his legs so he could save his energy to save me, and that he lost his claws defending secret knowledge.'

Misty snorted, 'Full of nonsense. And now not so full of life.'

Conker gasped, 'You mean...?'

'I mean, it's lucky that I already know his name. I don't like birds.'

'I really don't know what happened to him ... he was okay,' Conker mewed, 'There's a lot I don't understand. This is the first time I've been in The Outside. I came from The Boxes and Soggy has been helping me get back.'

'The Boxes?' Misty tipped her head to one side.

Conker nodded, 'It's a human place. I am a Ratter. I live there, with other Ratters.'

'And humans?' Misty asked.

'Yes.'

'Why?'

'They give us food ... if we catch the Ratbots. And we live there. There's no rain, or mud or wind. And it's warm. There's no...'

'No freedom, no freshness, no purity, no life!' Misty meowed.

Conker shook his head, 'I don't understand'. *Is she right...?* There was so much in The Outside that he'd never seen in The Boxes. *Wind... rain... trees...*

'Look at this place, young Ratter.' Misty hauled herself back up onto the wheel and waved her tail around at the piles of bent and rusted trucks. Conker gazed around, squinting at their harsh angles and jagged edges. 'Look at all the broken human things. This was once a beautiful valley ... a valley that held the warmth of the sun in its swathes of bright green grass and fruit laden gorse. A valley that spun the breeze around supple saplings and soft bracken dens... It was once the home of the Hill Cats....

'I was born in the den of the Glaring of Lairs. A den that is now filled with detritus and buried below this.' She tapped the wheel with her paw, and continued, 'My mother was Mara'raim Siki, Lucy, a stray from the Ward of Shady Ly, who long ago escaped to these hills with her mate, the Runner, Mik'piar Emer, Minty. I was named Misty when the humans trapped me and took me away from here. I got my Father Names when I escaped and found my way back. But by then it was too late. The hills had gone. The Glaring of Lairs had gone. All the Glarings had gone, except this one...'

Conker bowed his head. As he studied the greasy globs of putrid mud that clung to his fur, he tried to imagine the beautiful valley she'd described, but he could not.'

Misty went on, 'You must understand that the humans and the ... things ... they discard, are killing everything. The grass, the mice, the trees, the bugs, the birds ... and us. Life is broken. There is no food. There is no clean water. We fight and fool our friends and foes, demeaning ancient laws, just to keep our bellies full of rotting trash as we wait to die within these encroaching walls of creeping decay. We're all that's left of The Glaring of Ghosts. And my ghosts are all that remains of the Hill Cats. They linger for me now, impatient for my approaching death, desperate for my final decision.

'They may feed you now, and keep you trapped within their boxes, but look closer, Conker, and you will see that humans too will succumb to their own destruction.' she climbed down from the wheel and faced him again, 'So, what will you do when the humans have gone?'

'I ... I don't—'

A loud cawing cry interrupted him. Conker looked up to see a large black bird spiralling haphazardly downwards through the sparse branches. It landed heavily on top of a broken truck and fluttered its wings. Conker stared in amazement. It had a broken wing. It was the same bird that had been in the tree where he'd first met Soggy.

Misty thrashed her tail. 'We will talk more and attend to Soggy after I have dealt with this bird.'

'Good nightfall, Misty,' cawed the bird, 'I have answered your favour.'

Misty hissed as she clambered back onto the wheel and glowered at the bird, 'You most certainly have not, Stephen. May you be reminded of the peace amongst the Hosts. Retrieving a name is no favour for your kind, it is a fair law of Ganlengan, and you, as you know, will gain your fair reward for obeying it.'

'Both of them?' Stephen cawed.

'You may take only the departed, and only after you have delivered his name and we have guided his soul to our ghosts,' Misty growled, 'Soggy is not dead yet!'

'I can wait?' the Raven croaked.

Conker felt his stomach knot. *Yet...?* He looked at Soggy. The little tom was barely moving.

Misty took a deep breath, 'Do you have a name for the departed, Stephen?'

Stephen fluttered his good wing. 'As cried by a human child the night they left her beloved cat behind, Y hanow eis, Tinsel.'

'Thank you, Stephen,' Misty mewed. Then, as the raven thrashed his wings and flapped chaotically back up into the branches, she flicked her tail and yowled, 'GATHER FOR TINSEL!'

'You can stay here with Soggy,' Mellow whispered, 'you don't need to sing with us.'

'Sing?' Conker tipped his head, 'I'm sorry, I just don't understand any of this...'

'Misty speaks the ancient language of the birds. They are obliged to answer any request she makes in their tongue,' Mellow purred, 'She asked them to find the dead cat's name, that's all. Birds move in flocks, they are everywhere, and they hear everything. So, one of them will have heard this cat's name at some time. It's always the ravens or crows, or magpies that bring the names back to us, because they speak our language.'

'Why do you need his name?' Conker asked.

'To call his soul,' Crispy dipped his head, 'then we sing to call our ghosts and they invite him to linger with them. He doesn't have to. He can accept the choices offered by Shadow White, but the Glaring of Ghosts will give a cat the choice not to choose.'

Conker nodded, 'Thank you.' He still didn't understand, but he felt more at ease.

'Mellow, Crispy,' Misty mewed, 'talk later.'

The two toms dipped their head to Conker and hopped up onto the wheel, taking up their positions on either side of Misty. Conker padded around Soggy and crouched down beside him, curling his forelegs under the little tom's head, and wrapping his tail over his quarters. His breathing was shallow and the heat from his body felt like the sun on his face. Then he rested his head on the cold dead leaves beside the wheel and listened as Misty began to speak.

'Bow your heads. Listen to the sounds around you. The creak of the tree. The whine of the metal. The roar of the wind. Push them away. Listen again. The tap of the raven's claw. The air in your chest. Your heart in your ears. Throw those sounds aside. Open your mind.'

Conker's fur prickled. He remembered Gloworm saying something like this to Dust. So, he listened, and he did as Misty said, as Gloworm had said. He caught each sound that fell upon his ears and hurled them to the far corners of his mind. Then he listened again.

Misty went on, 'Tinsel, in your death you have found the Glaring of Ghosts. Tinsel, you will be offered a choice that Shadow White will not give. Tinsel, you can now choose not to choose, and wait with our ghosts who linger away from Ganlengan...

Conker closed his eyes and slowed his breathing until he could hear nothing but the echo of Misty's voice around the den, and the shift of her fur as she stood and began to sing...

'You only cast your shadows on my soul.'

Conker flicked an ear as Mellow stood, and after a pause, sang his line...

'My lonely tears are singing as they roll.'

Then Misty and Mellow took a breath and sang their lines again in quick succession...

'You only cast your shadows on my soul.'
'My lonely tears are singing as they roll.'

...Then they bowed their heads and took another breath. When they raised their heads again and sang on, Crispy added his own line after theirs...

'You only cast your shadows on my soul.'
'My lonely tears are singing as they roll.'
'I'm grieving and imagine you are whole.'

As Conker listened to their solemn voices, he took a slow deep breath and let it fall slowly from his jaws. Comforted by the warmth of Soggy's body, he felt himself falling deeper into the cold ground beneath him. The Glaring of Ghosts hung their heads. A deathly silence gripped the den, and when they all breathed deep and repeated their song again and again, Conker heard faint eerie voices prowling around the edges of his mind, stalking in and out of the soothing words in his ears, before reaching out to him and creeping deep into his open mind...

'You only cast your shadows on my soul.'
I feel your life so hauntingly
'My lonely tears are singing as they roll.'
I'm broken if I'm all you see
'I'm grieving and imagine you are whole.'

I feel your life so hauntingly
'You only cast your shadows on my soul.'
I'm broken if I'm all you see

'My lonely tears are singing as they roll.'
You only need remember me
'I'm grieving and imagine you are whole.'
Hear my heart and final plea
Quiet your song to let me be

I feel your life so hauntingly
I'm broken if I'm all you see
'You only cast your shadows on my soul.'
You only need remember me
Hear my heart and final plea
'My lonely tears are singing as they roll.'
Quiet your song to let me be
I feel your life so hauntingly
'I'm grieving and imagine you are whole.'
I'm broken if I'm all you see
You only need remember me
Hear my heart and final plea
Quiet your song to let me be

14
The Third Trial

'Soggy?'

Conker nudged the little tom's shoulder. He didn't move.

The Glaring of Ghosts had finished their song. The raven, Stephen, had taken Tinsel's body and the den was quiet except for the creaking and groaning of rusted metal and withered trees. Misty was grooming on the wheel, Mellow and Crispy dozed on the muddy leaves below her, with their heads on their paws.

'Conker?' Soggy flicked an ear.

'You're awake!' Conker shifted to let Soggy raise his head.

'Just ... about ... did I miss anything.'

'Nothing you need to worry about,' Misty hopped stiffly off the wheel and padded to Soggy's side, 'Now, sit yourself up, if you can.'

Soggy winced as he shifted his legs, 'I need my stick...?'

'Stick?' Misty mewed, 'What do you need a stick for?'

Conker looked around. He'd been carrying the stick for Soggy. But somewhere between following Wellington and entering the den, he'd lost it.

'It's magic...' Soggy winced again as he tried to raise himself into a sit, but he hadn't the strength, and slumped back down.

Misty caught his scruff in her jaws and steadied him. Then she let it go and shook her head, 'You don't need sticks, you need water. Clean water, and fast.'

'I need to get to The Sign.'

'The only place you'll be going without water is that raven's nest.'

Conker leant forward and licked Soggy's ear, 'Drink some water, then I can carry you to The Sign,' he sighed, 'If he can travel that far. Or I can go alone of you tell me where to find it.'

'Wait...! You must ... complete the ... Third Trial...' Soggy groaned.

'We can still get to The Sign,' Conker leapt to his paws, 'I can still carry you. Where is it? we should go...'

'I don't know...'

'You don't know?' Conker gasped.

'The Third Trial...'

'Enough!' Misty growled, 'He needs water, not signs, or sticks, or trials. Mellow, Crispy, get ready to fetch water. Our new friend Conker will be going with you.'

Conker glanced at the toms. Mellow's eyes were wide and Crispy's fur was rising slowly along is spine. *What is so frightening about getting water...?* He looked at the muddy floor. There was water everywhere, even if it did have a foul scent.

'You must ... pass the Third Trial...' Soggy took a deep breath and winced as he pushed himself up and mewed,

'A forlorn song ends,
'To rescue them from fading,
'With a dying friend.'

Then he slumped back down and closed his good eye.

Misty pressed a paw to is neck. 'Enough of this nonsense. This cat needs water, before that raven comes back.'

Mellow padded to Misty's side, 'We will go now,' he nodded to Conker, 'Come on, I'll explain on the way.'

As Mellow led the toms out of the den, Conker thought about the Third Trial. He guessed that a lonely song referred to the Shadow Song, but the rest of the riddle made no sense. *To rescue them from fading... did he mean the ghosts...? Do ghosts fade...? With a dying friend...? Does he mean himself...?*

'Getting fresh water is difficult,' Mellow mewed as they padded through the sticky mud of the gloomy lane, 'But it will be easier with you helping.'

Conker purred, 'Thank you, but I don't understand why we must fetch it. There's water everywhere.'

The ground here has poison in it,' Crispy mewed as he caught up, it makes everything sick. Many cats died before Misty realised this.'

Mellow stopped and turned to Conker, 'Misty died too.'

'She died?' Conker tipped his head.

'She has died from the poison many times,' Mellow mewed, 'But every time she dies, she chooses to return so she can keep singing the Shadow Song.'

Choose to return...? Conker shivered and licked his damp fur. *Rain...* 'What about the rain? Is the rain poisoned too?'

'The rain is safe,' Crispy purred, 'but it takes skill to catch it on your tongue. When it touches the ground, it becomes poison.'

'Soggy is in no state to catch the rain,' Mellow added, 'and the den is sheltered. We must fetch water as we fetch food.'

'From where?' Conker asked.

'From the dump... It's this way.' Mellow flicked his tail for Conker to follow and padded across the lane to the mouldering hedge. Crispy following solemnly.

Conker followed the toms in silence as they pushed through a narrow gap in the hedge. It was different from the hole he'd walked through with Soggy and Winter. No fresh green leaves or biting thorns here. Here, the flaky branches snapped, and wilted brambles slouched over their backs and clung to their fur as they walked.

Mellow and Crispy stopped on the other side of the hedge. In front of them a tall barrier made of trap metal rose high above their heads and expanded into the distance in both directions. Beyond it lay vast mountainous heaps of broken and mangled human things. His eyes hurt just looking at them. Conker clamped his jaws shut, not wanting to taste any of the rancid scents that flowed across the barrier. Everywhere he looked, giant white birds swooped and dived in and out of the festering heaps, and everywhere, the shadows shifted, as if something was moving below the rubbish. He narrowed his eyes and watched a bird as it flew away towards a distant undulating hill, then another, as it soared up from the heaps and circled above a row of scruffy brown boxes. Humans in impossibly bright coverers milled around them, and outside the nearest box, lounged two giant black and brown dogs.

'What is this place?' Conker padded to the mesh barrier and touched it with a paw.

'The dump,' Mellow mewed, 'It's where the humans leave the things they no longer want. Which includes food. This is where we eat.'

Conker let his eyes fall back to the shifting shadows. *Rats...?* 'Why can't you hunt rats?' he asked.

'We don't know which ones have drunk the water. Rats come into our den to take the food we can't eat, and they drink water from the ground in front of us. They don't get sick like we do, and they know we can't hunt them... They carry their ills well.'

'But how do you know if the food here is safe?' Conker asked.

'Humans bring food here every day and it only gets to the den if we take it there.'

Conker shook his head. 'So, why don't you leave the den, find a place with safe water?'

Mellow dipped his head, 'Misty will not leave. The Hill Cats lived here even before the humans made their promise. When the hills were lost under mountains of human rubbish, it fell to Misty to protect the last remaining Glaring, the Glaring of Ghosts. Not even Shadow White can persuade her to leave her ghosts.'

Conker nodded, 'I understand, but I can't imagine how hard it must be to live here. The Boxes were never dangerous, there was always fresh water, and the humans gave us food.'

'The Outside is not like that, Conker,' Mellow sighed, 'We have our freedom to live as cats should. We are not imprisoned in boxes and fed by humans. But The Outside is dangerous. I have met cats who chose to live with humans, because as their pets, life is longer, easier, and more comfortable. But it comes at a cost, and the beauty of living a free life is the price. You see, a cat may survive for many more seasons trapped in a human box and fed human food, but they will never experience what it truly means to be alive.'

Conker nodded. The Boxes were nothing compared to the magnificence of The Outside. If it were not for Fern, he would never consider going back, but he knew he would need to be brave to live here. *Would Fern cope...?*

Mellow purred, 'You will get used to it, with time. And time is something that we don't have if we are to save Soggy.'

Conker looked back over the hills of rubbish, 'But I don't see any water.'

Mellow took a deep breath, then flicked an ear to the scruffy brown boxes. 'It's in the Dog Box.'

'It's easy to get food,' Crispy mewed, 'The dogs don't care if we take that, but they make sharing their water a difficult task.'

Conker tipped his head to one side. 'How?'

Crispy went on, 'When we need water, we visit the dogs and command them to share stories before Red Wind. They must do it, but they don't like to. These two are not as friendly as Wellington.'

'And it's getting harder,' Mellow added, 'We are running out of tales to share.'

Winter had been ferocious, until the mere mention of Red Wind had compelled her to still her jaws and lay down as a friend. She had been happy to sit with him and Soggy and share stories. Wellington had appeared monstrous but had respectfully carried Tinsel's body to the Glaring of Ghosts. They had both been friendly. He looked at the two black and brown dogs lying on the floor in front of the Dog Box. They were big, but they didn't appear any more terrifying than either Winter or Wellington. He turned to Mellow, 'Why aren't they friendly?'

'They have been brainwashed,' Crispy mewed, 'If the humans are there, they will obey their commands before the laws of Red Wind.'

Conker remembered how cruel the humans in The Old Place and The Boxes could be, but they still brought food and fresh water every day, and if he'd been injured, they healed his wounds. 'Will the humans help you? Can they give you water?'

Crispy gasped, 'No. They don't help cats...'

'The humans here don't like us,' Mellow added, 'They chase us away. Some are safe, I know, but I still wouldn't risk approaching these humans. At least we know how to handle dogs.'

Conker nodded, 'Because we can share stories with them?'

'Dogs understand their promise and they respect the laws of Ganlengan. I'm not sure humans do anymore.' Mellow shook his head, 'So we will share with the dogs. Crispy will call Red Wind and you and I will find a way to carry the water back to Soggy. We've never needed to carry water back before. So, we will have to work it out quickly.'

'We get through the fence just over there,' Mellow flicked his tail as he padded along the barrier. Crispy followed. Conker padded behind them, one ear on the huge white birds and the other on the clink and chime of the fence as it moved in the wind. Before long they came to a place where it had been pulled from the ground and bent upwards, leaving a gap below it.

Mellow stopped and looked back, 'Crispy, are you ready?'

'I will try and make the story long, so you have more time,' Crispy mewed as he ducked under the fence and slipped away into the piles of rubbish.

Carrying water... A thought occurred to Conker, 'A bubble! The Green Female in The Boxes, she used a bubble to bring us water.'

'A bubble?' Mellow tipped his head, 'I'm not sure what you mean, but we can look...' He slipped through the hole, 'Let's see if we can find one.'

Conker's paws sunk deep into the rubbish as he followed Mellow. Foul stench filled his nostrils as colourful torn covers caught his paws, and shredded boxes and bowls fell against his legs. He kept his eyes open for a bubble, and it was not long before he saw one. It was crushed. But then he saw another, and another. They were everywhere. 'Mellow,' he mewed, 'wait, I see bubbles.'

Mellow stopped and watched with interest as Conker pawed through the rubbish and pulled out a crumpled and torn bubble. 'Of course! A bottle.'

'A what?' Conker peered into it.

'That's what the humans call them,' Mellow padded back to Conker's side and tapped the bottle with a paw, 'it will work, if we can find one that isn't broken.'

Together the toms scratched through the rubbish. They found many bottles. Most were too damaged to use, but finally they found one that was intact. Conker gripped its narrow top in his jaws and followed Mellow back out of the rubbish and onto the narrow muddy track that led around the back of the Dog Box. As Mellow slowed his pace and flicked his tail for him to hang back, Conker heard Crispy telling his story.

'...The song is called 'Shadow Song', and it's very old. As old as the hills...'

Stealthily, Mellow and Conker slipped into the shadows behind the dog box and began padding slowly along the wall.

'...Misty's mother, Lucy, joined the Hill Cats a long time ago, with her mate, Minty. It didn't matter that they had both been born in human houses, the Hill Cats still welcomed them and taught them their ways...'

As they approached the end of the wall, Mellow stopped and peered around the corner. His tail quivered and he took a step back before flicking an ear to invite Conker to follow.

'...You see, the thing about the Hill Cats, is that they never agreed with Shadow White's rules and choices...'

Conker caught sight of the rump of one of the dogs as they rounded the corner. It was almost as big as Wellington's, but with smooth fur and a stump for a tail. He felt his stomach drop. *Where did its tail go...?*

'...They believed the choices are unfair as a cat is forced to choose...'

'*...So, the Hill Cats defied Shadow White?*' a dog gruffed.'

'That's the only way in...' Mellow flicked his tail to a large hole in the side of the Dog Box.

Conker followed, keeping close to the wall. He could see the dogs clearly now.

'*...That's right,*' Crispy went on, '*They made a decree. Just after the rules and choices were delivered to the living oracles. The Glaring of Thorns called a meeting. The other Glarings, Lairs, Gales, Trees ... and the others ... there were lots, they all attended the meeting and decided that when a Hill Cat died, they should choose to make no choice...*'

Mellow slipped inside the Dog Box. Conker hurried in after him.

'*...So, they created the Glaring of Ghosts. A Glaring where their dead could linger together...*'

Dull light slid into the Dog Box through the jagged holes in the roof. Swirling motes of dust floated in the light. The pungent scent of dog overpowered the stench of the rubbish outside, and Conker was thankful for that.

'*...And the Glaring of Ghosts, they are still here?*' a dog woofed.

'*... Yes, Misty remains to protect them...*'

Mellow padded to the far corner of the Dog Box, 'The water bowl is here, try pushing the bottle into it, see if any water will go inside it.'

'*...And the Shadow Song? What does it do ... exactly...?*'

'*...It calls the ghosts of the Hill Cats, so they can invite the souls of the newly departed to linger with them...*'

Conker dropped the bottle into the water bowl and pressed it down gently with his paw. He was pleased to see a little trickle of water flow into it.

'*...And if she doesn't sing the Shadow Song ... what then? What will happen when Misty dies...?*'

'*...Misty always returns to keep singing...*'

Conker pressed down a little harder on the bottle as he listened. *A lonely song ends...* he recalled the ghostly voices that had answered the song, "*Quiet your song to let me be...*" *do the ghosts* want *the song to end...?*

'*...And what will happen when Shadow White refuses to let Misty return to her body?*' the dog woofed, '*Will she refuse the choices offered by her Host, and instead choose to linger with her ghosts? How will she protect them then? Every dog knows that a lingering ghost is lost to death. They forfeited their choices when they died and can never recall their Host to change their mind. They are trapped, fading with time in the living world. Then what will happen to the Glaring of Ghosts...?*'

'*...I think ... I...*'

Conker froze. His fur lifted along his spine.

'*...That's right little cat,*' wuffed the dog, '*The soul of every Hill Cat that ever lived will be lost forever...*'

To Rescue them from fading... Conker felt the water soak into his paw. *A dying friend... Misty... Quiet your Song to let me be...* The bottle slipped from under his paw. The air inside it bubbled out and broke on the surface of the water with a loud bloop.

'What was that?' growled a dog.

'Oh, no...' Mellow mewed.

Heavy paws scuffed the floor. Mellow backed into the corner of the Dog Box. Conker let the bottle bob in the bowl as he stepped back. A dark shadow fell across the doorway.

'Look Copper, more cats.'

'You're right Nickel, were going to have some fun today.'

The shadow deepened as the second dog poked its giant slavering jaws through the doorway.

Through their legs, Conker could see Crispy. His eyes wide, his fur raised, and his tail bushed.

15
Deadly Secrets

The half full bottle bobbed in the water bowl as Conker backed away. Copper padded into the Dog Box, his tongue lolling as he panted, dripping saliva onto his huge brown paws.

'They are friends!' Crispy meowed from behind the dogs.

Nickel turned to look at Crispy, 'Then why are they sneaking around in here?'

'They're not ... they are... they're just ... they—'

'Enough!' Nickel barked at Crispy. Then he turned back to Copper, 'Ask them what they are doing.'

Copper licked his jaws, 'Like he said, what are you doing?'

Mellow stepped forward. 'We have come to share tales with Red Wind.'

'All right,' Copper woofed, 'then follow me, and don't try to run. I get excited when I see cats running.'

'Do as they say,' Mellow mewed quietly as Copper backed out of the dog box and padded around Crispy. Nickel waited to make sure Mellow and Conker were following, then circled and padded after them.

Conker kept his head low as he found a dry spot and sat down next to Crispy. Mellow sat on the other side of the white tom.

Nickel paced back and forth behind the cats as Copper flopped down in front of them and gave his chin a good scratch, then he looked up at Nickel, 'I think we are being very generous allowing these cats to join us and share tales, don't you think brother?'

'Very generous. But that doesn't mean we are nice, or that we will be generous again. Red Wind does not care for the defiance of cats.'

Mellow dipped his head low, his nose almost touching the floor, 'Thank you brother's, you are very generous, and be assured that we are only here because we enjoy sharing tales with Red Wind as much as you do.'

'I hope that's true,' Nickel glanced at Copper, 'Now, Crispy has just finished telling the story of the Shadow Song.'

'Great story,' gruffed Copper.

'Great story' Nickel repeated as he looked from Mellow to Conker, then back to Mellow again, 'Not you,' he shook his head, 'We've heard plenty of your stories,' he looked back to Conker, 'You.'

Conker lifted his head a little, 'Me?'

'Yes, a big cat like you must have plenty of stories to tell. So, tell us your name and the story of the first lesson your mother ever taught you.'

Conker lifted his head and looked at the big dog, 'My name is Conker and my mother never taught me anything ... I never knew her.'

Copper snorted, 'I can see that you are a stranger around here, so let me explain Red Wind's law. I ask for a tale, and you tell it. No lies.'

Conker sighed, 'I think my full name is Black Conker, I heard the humans say that, and I know that some cats have Mother Names, but I don't. I never knew my mother.'

'Liar!' Nickel padded up behind Conker, 'All cats have Mother Names. All mother cats name their kittens as they are born. Don't try to fool us. You may be a big strong cat, but you are still small and weak to dogs like us.'

'I am not lying,' Conker got to his paws and turned to face Nickel. Crispy shifted uncomfortably at his side, Mellow remained motionless with his head down. 'I'm a Ratter, I was raised by humans.'

Nickel lowered his head, level with Conker's nose. 'Lots of cats are kept by humans. They still have mothers and Mother Names. A cat with no Mother Name is dead at birth.

'But...' Conker flicked his tail in annoyance. *Won't these dogs listen...?*

'I think,' Mellow lifted his head, 'That Conker was a prisoner of humans, perhaps they took him from his mother before she could name him.'

Nickel turned on Mellow, 'Had his mother not taught him how to breathe, he would be dead. That is a lesson.' He turned back to Conker, 'Tell me the story of *that* lesson.'

Conker dropped his head. He didn't have a single memory that could have been of his mother. He'd never even known that he might have had one until he met the other Ratters. He took a deep breath and looked up at Nickel, 'I am sorry, I just don't know.'

'If you are keeping your tale a secret, it would be a very dangerous secret to keep,' growled Copper.

'Copper, surely a smart dog like you must understand,' Mellow dipped his head, 'This cat has suffered at the hands of humans. He has escaped them. We all know how cruel humans can be, is it so hard to believe that they would take a cat from his mother and leave him nameless?'

'It's been a long time since you fled your own humans, Mellow,' Nickel growled. 'You want to believe him. But I say we give this cat one last chance to tell his tale, and if he does not, Red Wind will rise against you all.'

Conker held his breath as Copper stood and padded to his brother's side. As the two huge dogs stood rib to rib, staring down at him, his mind went blank. He shook his head, 'I'm sorry... I have many tales that I could tell about The Old Place or The Boxes...' he looked up, 'They are strange tales. Ones that you won't have heard before. But Mellow is right. The humans must have taken my mother away from me ... I just don't remember her.'

'Strange tales from a strange cat,' Copper gruffed, 'A cat who, without a mother, grew so big and strong.'

Mellow stood, leant into Conker's side, and flicked his tail for Crispy to get up.

The dogs kept their eyes on Conker.

'Big enough to insult Red Wind.' Nickel growled.

'Crispy ... get behind the Dog Box...' Mellow mewed.

Conker flicked his ear and listened to Crispy's paw steps as he leapt up and bounded away.

'Strong enough to run?' Copper gruffed, 'I do like a good chase.'

'Don't move...' Mellow mewed.

Conker flicked an ear to him as, side by side, the dogs took a step forward.

'When I yowl, follow me ... fast...'

'We do like a good chase,' don't we brother?' Nickel licked his jaws.

Conker could feel the dog's hot fetid breath ruffle his fur. *Soggy... How hot will he be now... he needs water...* Conker looked at the door to the dog box. The bottle bobbed in the water bowl.

'Oh yes, we do like a good chase...' Copper scratched the floor with his huge paw and rocked backwards.

'RUN!' Mellow flicked Conker with his tail as he turned and bounded for the Dog Box. Then he leapt, bounced off the wall and grabbed the jutting roof with his claws. As Conker turned to follow, the large ginger tom was already hauling himself up onto the roof. Conker leapt forward, just as Nickel's teeth snapped the air where his tail had been. Conker concentrated on the roof. The jump would be easy for him. *Water...* Mellow was moving back from the edge to give him room, but as he neared the wall, his legs didn't prop. He didn't take the jump. His mind steered him sideways and through the doorway.

'Conker, NO!' Mellow yowled.

Nickel and Copper collided in the doorway as Conker bounded through. He leapt the water bowl, slid to a halt behind it and turned to face the dogs. Nickel had pushed ahead of Copper and was padding through the door, his brown eyes trained on Conker.

Conker kept his eyes on the dogs as he pawed the bottle out of the bowl and picked it up in his jaws. He hadn't thought about how he'd get back out of the Dog Box. His only escape route was through their legs. He held the bottle tight in is jaws and watched their movements as they padded closer, waiting for his moment. Then something moved behind them.

'Crispy, get back,' Mellow mewed.

Crispy...? Conker's stomach tightened as he spotted Crispy's slim white legs fidgeting nervously behind the dogs.

Copper turned his head, 'You get the big one, I'll see to this scrawny one.'

'Crispy ... RUN!' Mellow yowled as Copper growled and turned on the white tom.

Conker watched in horror as Crispy scrabbled on the floor as he tried to turn. *He'll never outrun Copper...* Nickel loomed closer, his lips curled in a snarl.

With a yowl, Mellow dropped from the roof and landed on Nickel's back, and as the dog turned his head to snap, the ginger tom leapt off him and bounded away after Copper and Crispy.

Conker saw his chance. Before Nickel could turn his huge head back to him, he tightened his grip on the bottle and bounded forward, leapt onto the dog's head, and dug his claws deep into the fur on Nickel's neck. As the dog yelped and stumbled, Conker bounded down his back and leapt for the floor.

Mellow was ahead, gaining on Copper. He couldn't see Crispy but the dog was heading towards the hole in the fence. Conker raced forward, his long legs an advantage and he caught up with Mellow easily. He could see Crispy now, running as fast as he could for the hole, but he was slowing down. Copper was gaining on him.

'Distract ... the ... dog,' Mellow mewed as Conker drew level with him. As Conker nodded, more water spilled from the bottle in his jaws. He gripped it tighter and quickened his pace. Copper was just ahead of him on the path. He lunged forward and headbutted the dog on the hind leg. Copper stumbled sideways but didn't slow. Conker kept up with him, and as he drew level again, he leapt at his rump and dug his claws into his flank. Copper yelped and kicked out, catching Conker on the shoulder, but he still didn't slow down.

Mellow caught up again as Conker righted himself, and together they ran on after Crispy. Conker could hear Nickel's large paws thudding the floor behind them, gaining on them with every heavy step.

The fence rattled as Crispy crashed into it. Conker watched in horror as he tried to scramble under it, but Copper was quick. The dog clamped his jaws on Crispy's hind leg and pulled him back. Crispy yowled in pain.

Conker leapt onto Copper's Back and dug his claws deep into his shoulder. The dog dropped Crispy's leg and turned his head back to snap at him. Mellow dived past and helped Crispy crawl under the gap in the fence, his bitten hind leg trailing limply behind him.

Conker hung onto Copper's back as he looked around for somewhere to jump down, but Nickel had caught up and was circling his brother. There was nowhere he could land and get to the gap in the fence without risking being caught in their slavering jaws. He hung on tighter. Mellow's eyes went wide with horror as he watched from the other side of the fence, Crispy lay panting at his side. Conker looked up at the fence. *If I can leap onto that... If I can hang on... If I can climb it...* But as he studied the distance to the fence, he began to doubt he'd escape with all his legs.

Then something moved in the shadows.

Mellow flicked an ear in surprise as Misty slid out of the wilted grass, trudged stiffly to the hole, scrambled through it, and sat up tall before the dogs. Then she meowed softly.

'Not tonight,
'As Red Wind blows,
'We will not fight,
'Nor fear our foes,
'Tonight, we wash for Shadow White.'

Both dogs froze as she lifted a paw, licked it, and ran it over her ear. Mellow helped Crispy up, and together they licked their paws and ran them over their own ears.

Copper and Nickel stared down at Misty. Then Nickel gruffed, 'You're no fun, old Hill Cat.'

Conker leapt down from Copper's back and padded to Misty's side. He thought of Gloworm as he licked his own paw and ran it over his ear. He hoped he was doing it right.

Nickel and Copper looked at each other and shook their heads. Then they turned and padded back down the track towards the Dog Box.

16
The Sign

Misty pulled herself up onto the wheel and thrashed her tail. 'You failed to get any water. Crispy is injured. You insulted Red Wind and forced me to surrender to her in the name of Shadow White just to stop you all getting killed,' she glared at Conker.

Conker lowered his head.

'And ... you failed ... the Third Trial...' Soggy mewed weakly.

'Be quiet, Soggy,' Misty growled, 'Save your energy for getting to The Sign. It's your only hope now!'

The Sign... Conker lifted his head, 'I need to find The Sign. I need to—'

'No, you do not,' Misty interrupted, thrashing her tail again, 'It is Soggy who needs to find The Sign.'

'But I need to get back to The Boxes, back to Fern...'

'As you told this foolish little tom before he tricked you into taking *him* there.'

Conker looked at Soggy. The little tom looked barely able to move anywhere. He was slumped against the wheel, resting his head on Crispy. The empty bottle lay on the floor beside him. All but a drop of water that Conker had collected had been spilled as they'd run away from the dogs.

Soggy glanced up at Conker, then closed his good eye, 'It was ... no trick,' he sighed, 'Conker needs ... The Sign too ... to get back to ... Fern.'

'Conker just needed to get back in the truck, or wait until it returned,' Misty mewed.

'What?' Conker glanced at Misty, then glared at Soggy, 'You said it would never come back.'

'I said ... I hadn't seen one come back. But I ... hadn't been there long...'

'And you said that only doom and a certain meeting with The White Kitten awaited me.'

Soggy lifted his head a little, 'That is ... always a possibility...'

'But why? I needed to get back to Fern.'

Soggy sighed and pulled his new stick closer to him. He bit down onto it and winced as he shifted his tail over his hind legs, then dropped it again to meow, 'Misty's right. I ... I needed your help, Conker.'

Conker shook his head, 'I don't understand. You said you were helping me?'

'The Sign ... will ... get you home...'

'Enough!' Misty growled, 'Soggy, be quiet. I can tell him without all your nonsense.' She turned to Conker, 'Soggy stopped here yesterday. A lost stray trying to find his way home to his humans. I told him that if thats what he really wants, he should find The Sign and stop pestering us with his pointless riddles.'

'Trials...'

'Shhh!' Misty went on, 'Mellow offered to escort him to The Sign, but the silly tom insisted on finding some farm dog first. He'd heard her barking and wanted to partake in one of her Listenings. Something about an old dog friend of his. I told him it was impossible to get to the farms from here, as they are on the other side of the road, but he refused to listen, and wondered off insisting that he knows how to cross roads.'

Conker looked at Soggy, 'You said it cannot be crossed.'

'Shhh!' Misty hissed again before Soggy could speak and went on. 'At least he told the truth of that. Look what happened to him when he tried.'

Conker looked at Soggy. Pain coursed over his good eye as he bit down harder into his stick. His other eye had grown even larger, angry red, and weeping. His swollen tail was grotesquely bent and his legs lifeless and frail. He could barely curl his clawless paws. Conker's stomach dropped like a stone. *That's why he was so afraid...* 'The trucks, they caught you...? You died?'

'Not quite...'

'Not yet,' Misty growled, 'Conker, you must take him to The Sign before he does. Mellow will guide you there while I attend to Crispy's wound. Luckily it isn't too deep, just a wrench with holes in it.'

'Not until ... he passes ... the Third Trial...'

'Oh, do stop talking, Soggy. You will go to The Sign now!

A lonely song ends... Conker lifted his head, 'Wait, I have solved the riddle. I haven't failed the Third Trial.'

'Really?' Soggy tried to lift his head.

'The Shadow Song. The dogs ... what they said to Crispy.'

Misty thrashed her tail, 'What did they say to Crispy?'

'They said, the ghost of every Hill Cat that ever existed will be lost forever.'

Misty shook her head, 'And what would a dog know?'

Conker took a breath and sat down, 'I have the answer to the Third Trial. Misty, you must stop singing the Shadow Song.'

'And who are you to tell me what to do!' Misty growled.

Conker glanced at Mellow. The ginger tom looked up from licking the wound on Crispy's hind leg and nodded. Conker went on, 'Soggy's third trial was:

'A forlorn song ends,
'To rescue them from fading,
'With a dying friend.'

'And what nonsense is that?'

Conker shuffled uncomfortably under the she-cat's glare, 'Misty, when you sang the Shadow Song, I heard other voices.'

Her eyes widened, 'You did?'

'I opened my mind, as you said. I pushed the sounds aside. There is a Ratter in The Boxes, his name is Gloworm, I remember him telling Dust how to do this. He said "Close your eyes and concentrate on the noises around you ... then separate them. Stretch your mind and push the noises apart, just enough to let in a little bit more ... and more of your memories will slip through the gaps in the noise."'

'Memories?' Misty sniffed as she clambered down from the wheel and padded to Conker, 'That is how you invite the ghosts to speak, not how you find your memories...' She shook her head, 'What did they say?'

Ghosts... Conker closed his eyes as he tried to recall their words. And as they slowly crept back into his mind, he repeated them quietly to Misty:

'I feel your life so hauntingly,
'I'm broken if I'm all you see,
'You only need remember me,
'Hear my heart and final plea,
'Quiet your song to let me be,'

Misty sat down and hissed.

Conker opened his eyes and spoke gently to the old she-cat. 'I don't know much about The Outside, but Soggy's trial makes sense to me now. The forlorn song is the Shadow Song, and you sing it to keep the ghosts of the Hill Cats close to you. But what if one day Shadow White refuses to let you return to your body? Who will sing it then? And if you refuse to make a choice and linger with your ghosts, how will you ever call upon Shadow White again. You and your ghosts will be lost forever. Fading with time, like the dogs said.'

'I have Mellow and Crispy to sing the Shadow Song. I trust them with my soul and my ghosts.'

'I don't doubt that, but what if they cannot stay here. You said yourself the earth is poisoned with human rubbish. What if they are forced to move away from you and your ghosts?'

'They will find a way.'

'You must save your ghosts, Misty,' Conker looked up into the old she-cat's glistening eyes, 'Because you are the dying friend.'

She shook her head, 'For a stranger, you sound very certain of everything.'

'Misty...' Mellow mewed sadly.

You said it yourself, Conker went on, "My ghosts, they linger for me, impatient for my approaching death,"

'Told ... you...' Soggy mewed, 'Will you ... believe me ... now a stranger ... sees your ... problem?'

Misty thrashed her tail, 'Be quiet, Soggy.'

'He's right, isn't he?' Mellow padded to Misty's side and licked her ear. 'I can see you are struggling. You will die again soon, won't you?'

Misty hung her head, 'I don't have long. And yes, there is a risk that Shadow White could refuse to grant my choice to return...'

'So, we will be alone?' Crispy mewed weakly, 'Here?'

'Conker is right,' Mellow mewed, 'Look at this place, Misty. The humans bring more rubbish every day. Soon there will be no more here. We are already sick and starving. We will not be able to fool Nickel and Copper so easily now. We will soon need to find a new home, and to do that, we will have no choice but to leave the ghosts.'

Crispy pulled himself up onto his forelegs, 'But where would we go?'

'Winter!' Conker sat up and purred, 'She said she'd welcome some cats on her farm, to hunt the ... the...'

'Mice...' mewed Soggy.

'Mice...' Mellow purred.

'But how can we get there?' Crispy asked.

'The pipe under the road is clear.' Conker went on, 'The rats who lived there asked me to look after it when they left to find the Rat King. You can look after it now and use it to get to Winter's farm.'

Misty stared at Conker until the den fell silent, then dropped her head and mewed quietly, 'Then it is decided.

The ancient territories of the Hill Cats have been decimated by humans and their detritus. This is no longer a safe place for any cat to live. The Glaring of Ghosts will die with me. When I meet Shadow White again, I, along with the lingering ghosts of the Hill Cats will accept her invitation and enter Warkiersu. And my loyal friends, Mellow and Crispy will be free to start a new life as farm cats.'

'Thank you, Misty,' Mellow purred.

Crispy echoed, 'Thank you.'

Soggy shifted awkwardly, 'Well done ... Conker, you have passed ... the Third ... Trial.'

'Shut up, Soggy!' Misty hissed.

Conker lowered his head. He was relieved that he'd solved the riddle, but he could feel Misty's sadness. Winter was a kind-hearted dog and would welcome Mellow and Crispy. He just hoped that Shadow White would welcome the stubborn old she-cat as readily.

'But I am not dead yet!' Misty straightened herself, 'And neither, surprisingly, is this tenacious little tom.'

'Shall I ... tell ... Shadow White ... that you are ... on your way?'

'You will do no such thing!' Misty hissed. 'Conker, Mellow, get this cat to The Sign. Regardless of the ruin humans have caused, they are still *his* only hope of survival. The Sign is one place where a few good humans still exist. I hope they can patch him up and send him back to where he belongs.'

'It's been ... nice ... knowing you too, Misty,' Soggy purred.

'Yes, yes, now go before I decide to call that raven.'

Conker waited as Soggy said his goodbyes to Misty and Crispy. Then he crouched down as Mellow helped drag the little tom over his back and offered him his stick.

'What's the stick for?' Mellow asked.

'It's ... magic,' Soggy purred, 'When I bite it ... the pain... disappears.'

Conker purred. *It banishes the things I don't like...* When Soggy was comfortable, Conker said his own goodbyes. He wished Crispy a quick recovery and promised that when he escaped The Boxes again, he and Fern would come and join them on Winter's farm. He thanked Misty for everything he'd learned and promised to put the knowledge to good use. And he vowed to keep her story alive, until the day he met Shadow White himself.

He took one last look back as he followed Mellow out of the den. Crispy was resting comfortably beside the wheel. Misty had climbed back onto it and was sat with her head raised and eyes closed, her jaws moving gently as if singing a silent song.

As Conker followed Mellow along a narrow uphill path at the side of a withered hedge, he noticed that the ginger tom's outline was beginning to darken. He blinked, and as he did, the sky lightened around them. He gazed up into the soft grey clouds. The moon was falling and dimming, something else was brightening up The Outside.

He could barely feel Soggy's weight on his back. The little tom was hot and fidgety. Conker kept his pace steady, as he could no longer feel the little tom's claws.

Mellow stopped at the top of the hill and beckoned Conker with his tail. Conker caught up and side by side the toms looked down into the valley below. To one side, Conker could see the dump's vast mountains of rubbish and ramshackle boxes, enclosed in the endless mesh fence they had climbed through not long before. To the other side, soft green hills rolled gently into one another, like ripples on a fresh bowl of water. Trees sprang up randomly all over them, some stood alone, others in groups. Narrow hedges cut the hills into squares as they wove across them. Further along the path, and not too far away, a cluster of shadowy yet pleasant looking human boxes sat enclosed in neat patches of grass and earth. Shiny trucks rested all around them. The tallest box was light coloured and stood proud under a huge leafy tree. Conker took a deep breath as he recalled Misty's description of the valley before the rubbish came. 'Where are we?' he asked.

'Watch,' Mellow purred.

Conker let his eyes follow Mellow's ears to the distant hills. The dark sky was lightening into a soft pale blue just above them. And as he watched, an intense golden light broke out of the ground and spilled down into the valley, scattering the shadows and the cold and the damp with its bright fierce light. *The sun...!* And Just as the light of the rising sun flooded the valley, the rain began to fall again, shimmering this time, glistening cool and warm in the sunlight. Conker looked up in astonishment as a band of brilliant colours appeared suddenly and arced across the paling sky.

All over the valley, soft hazy mists began to rise from the undulating grass, and everywhere his eyes landed, bright colourful flowers were unfolding. Conker blinked and stared as the gentle light flooded The Outside, warming it, brightening it, and when it had reached the tallest human box, it washed up the walls and lit up three bright green shapes. One was the shape of a cat.

'The Sign,' Mellow purred, 'The humans here are safe. They care for cats and dogs, and other creatures too.'

Conker looked up at The Sign. He could make out the shape of a dog too, but there was a third shape he didn't recognise, 'What's the other creature?' he asked.

'That's a rabbit.'

'Winter said she could handle the rabbits...' Conker studied the shape ... 'what's wrong with its ears?'

Mellow purred, 'Have you ever seen one?'

'No,' Conker twitched his whiskers.

'That's because they have the best ears. They will hear you coming before you even find their scent. You could leave Soggy on the step below The Sign. He will be fine, and if you like, I could teach you how to track rabbits on the way to Winter's farm?'

Conker shook his head, 'I will wait with Soggy. I need to go back to The Boxes. I can escape again and bring Fern with me, maybe the other Ratters too, if they want to come.'

Mellow dropped his head, 'If you are sure that you will find her. These humans are kind, but I don't know where they take cats.'

'I know I will find her, because of what my friend Brook told me.'

'Brook?' Mellow mewed, 'What did she tell you.'

'She said, 'If you ever lose anything dear to you, keep a door forever open in your heart, so it knows it will always be welcome back.'

Mellow purred, 'That sounds like something my mother told me. I am sure you will find Fern. Good luck, Conker, I hope to see you again soon.'

Mellow gave Soggy's ear a lick and mewed quietly, 'Good luck to you too, I hope you find your home.' Then he turned at padded back down the hill towards the last remaining territory of the ancient Hill Cats.

My mother...? Conker felt a warm bubble burst in his chest. It warmed is heart, then his mind, and even his cold muddy feet as he began padding down the path towards The Sign. *Was Brook my mother...?*

17
The Trap

'*Dontmove.*'

Conker tensed as he felt the female human's hand on his back. He turned his head and saw green covers and long brown head fur. She reminded him of Fiona.

'*Thisonelooksokay, whataboutthatone.*'

Soggy lay on the cold stone step next to him. He was burning hot and hadn't moved since Conker had helped him gently down from his back. A second human, a male, bent over him and scooped him up into his arms.

'*Notgoodemma, illgethiminsideandonadrip, hehassome nastyinjuries.*'

Conker relaxed as the female human lifted him up over her shoulder. *They're going to help...*

'*howdoyouthinktheygothere.*'

'*Wellthebigtabbyismuddyandwet, excepthisback, andthe littletomisonlywetononeside, maybehecarriedthelittle one.*'

'*Carriedhim, seriouslyjames.*'

'*Whynot cats areweird.*'

Conker tipped his head back as they were carried through a large brown door and into a long bright box. The roof was made of white squares, and the walls were a fresh pale green. It was cleaner and more refreshing than the Meeting Box, but it still reminded him of home.

The male human half turned to push open a door with his shoulder and backed into a smaller box. Conker sighed with relief as he saw Soggy's eye flick open for a heartbeat. *He's alive...* but it closed again as the male human laid him down gently on a ledge.

'*Fingerscrossed*,' the male human uttered as he picked up a long object with a large circle at one end and waved it over Soggy. It beeped.

'*Hehasachip.*'

'*Goodwhataboutthisone.*'

The female human lifted Conker onto the ledge, and the male human waived the object in the air over him. It beeped again.

'*Thatsgood.*'

'*Hehasaneartattooaswell,*

'*Thatsunusual,*' the male human gently took hold of Conker's ear and peered at it, *Iwillgettheinjuredonestable, hecangoinacagewhileyoucontacttheowners.*'

'*Sure*,' she hoisted Conker up over her shoulder. He relaxed as she carried him out of the small box and back into the long bright box. As the door closed behind them, Conker saw the male human taking strange shiny objects out of hidden compartments. *Please be okay, Soggy...*

Conker was carried into another, identical box full of traps. The female human lifted him carefully into a trap and gave him a gentle fuss before she closed the door. There was a small water bowl in the trap, and he purred as his paws touched the soft covers on the floor. It was familiar and he needed the rest.

'Thereyougojustrestinthere.'

Conker padded a few circles and flopped down onto the dry warm bed. He hadn't slept since he'd escaped the truck, and even though he already missed the fresh patches of air, and the wind and the rain of The Outside, if felt good to get back to a warm comfortable bed. As he lapped at the cool fresh water, he thought of Misty. *Was she right? How can humans give one cat fresh water, and poison the home of another...?*

The female human sat down at a ledge and began moving objects around in front of her. Conker pricked his ears as she picked one up, prodded it, then began talking to it. Her kind voice was comforting, and as he listened to her indecipherable words broken occasionally by their names, he felt his eyes become heavy. He was almost asleep when the door opened, and the male human walked in.

'Anyluck.'

'Yestheblackandwhitetomiscalled Soggy andhesbeen reportedmissingbytheowner, ihavetheirdetails. Thetabbyisa Ratter, numberfourtysix, hesaworkingcat ownedbyratevict.

Conker lifted his head.

'Ratevict, isntthatwherefionaworksnow.'

'Ithinkso, illcallthemaftericall Soggy's owner.'

'Okayletmeknowwhattheysay, heneedssurgeryassoonaspossible.'

Conker dropped his head back onto his paws and listened as the male human left the box and the female human began talking to the objects again...

'Helloisthatmrslovett ... hiitsemmafromhillsidevets ... yes ... wehave Soggy here ... yes ... yesheisok ... onmy thatisalongtime... wellheisstablebuthehassomeinjuriesand *thatneed treatmenturgently ... ohthatsgreatblessyou ... ofcoursewewill ... doyouknowhereweare ... ohthatsgreat...*

Conker woke with a start. The male human was at the other side of the box, closing a trap door. He could see Soggy inside the trap, tightly bound in white covers. After the male human had left, Conker tried calling to him, but the little tom didn't answer, so he climbed up the bars of his own trap to get a better look. The little tom looked fast asleep, his chest rising and falling steadily. His fur was clean and dry, and his wounds were all covered. *He's alive... they've healed him...* Conker forced himself to lie down and rest. *He'll wake up soon... I'm sure he will...* He wondered if Soggy was as tired and hungry as he was...

He awoke again to the scent of food on his tongue. His mouth began to water. He lifted his head to see that a small bowl of dry nuggets had been put in the trap next to him. It seemed like ages since he'd shared the rat with Soggy. He looked across at the other trap. The little tom was still sleeping, still breathing steadily.

'*Howarethey*' The male human entered the box.

'The Ratter *isdoinggreat hesjusthungryandtired,* Soggy *hasntwokenup.*'

The male human sighed heavily and shook his head, '*Ihopehemakesit.*

'*Ivejustspokentohisowner, hehasbeenmissingforayear, sincetheirold dog died, thekidsaresoexcitedthathesbeen found, butitoldherhisinjuriesaresevere.*' The female sighed, '*Andicalledratevict,* 'Theirrepresentative ... craigfrost, willbe *heresoonsowebetterget Brauntreo Black Conker, imean, Ratter numberfourtysix,readytogo.'*

'Lethimeatfirst, hewontgetmuchsherehesgoing, theycan wait,' the male added as he left the box again.

Conker dozed again after eating all the dry nuggets. His stomach was full and aching. He didn't think he'd ever eaten this much food before in his life. The Boxes in The Sign were quiet. Soggy had stirred in his sleep and mumbled about trials and sticks and dogs and roads, but he still hadn't woken properly. Conker was worried about him, and he was sure the humans were too. They came back to look at him frequently, their fear scent rising as they spoke gently to him. They'd paid little attention to Conker, but he felt fine, and as his stomach began to ease after his big meal, The Sign began to fill with voices. Humans were talking loudly.

Suddenly, the door burst open and a male in white covers barged into the room and slammed a heavy trap down on the ledge, '*Whereisit,*' he growled.

'The Ratter isinthecagethere.'

The white male's face appeared on the other side of the bars and sneered at Conker with cold blue eyes. Conker shifted backwards as he growled, *'Timetogobackwhere youbelong, anddontthinkyouwilleverbegettingoutagain.'*

'Conker?' Soggy groaned.

Conker leapt forward, 'Soggy! You're awake.'

'I ... er... Conker? Where are we?'

'At The Sign. The humans healed you, but I have to go back to The Boxes now.'

The trap door opened, and the white male thrust his hand in and grabbed Conker by the scruff, gripped it tightly and dragged him out of the trap. Conker tried to fight him, but his grip was too strong, and too painful. He felt helpless, but as he was hoisted into the air, he caught a glimpse of the little tom, staring up at him with one bright wide eye. And as he was stuffed into another dark trap, Conker heard Soggy meow, 'Thank you ... my friend.'

Then the cage door slammed shut. And as the blanket fell over the trap, Conker closed his jaws to the stench of sour damp, his ears to the clang of metal and his eyes to the stifling darkness, and he imagined he was sitting in the long grass beside Fern, as she listened to her first rustle of leaves, felt her first raindrop soak into her fur, and watched her first sun rise over The Outside.

www.ghostsofshadyly.com

Misty

You only cast your shadows... My lonely tears are singing... I'm grieving ... imagine... Misty blinked open her eyes.

Shadow White hung her head. Her gentle glow dimmed, revealing hundreds of pairs of brightly glowing eyes. The bright eyes flashed and blinked as they slowly drew nearer and formed a circle around Misty.

As the White Kitten raised her head again, her glow brightened, and the eyes of the ghosts faded away. 'Meo'Keo, Orar'Rai, Mik'emer Piar, Misty. Have you changed your mind?'

Misty dipped her head, 'I will never agree with you, Uimywim, but humans have left the Hill Cats no choice. In you, at least, a cat will find solace.'

'And I extend my invitation to every cat, regardless of their opinions. Warkiersu welcomes the collective knowledge of the magnificent Hill Cats. But I am intrigued, who persuaded this ever tenacious she-cat to reconsider her options? Was it Mellow, or Crispy? Or clever little Soggy? I am sure he would have seen your ... predicament.'

'Soggy? Is he...?'

'No, not ... yet.'

'Good .... I do hope that irksome little tom found his way home. And it was none of them. It was the cat who *carried* Soggy who helped me see ... other possibilities.'

'The cat who carried him?' Uimywim tipped her head to one side.

'He called himself Conker, but he had no mother name. He told us he was an escaped Ratter, previously imprisoned by humans, and had never been outside before.'

'A Ratter?' Uimywim shook her head, 'and you say he *carried* Soggy. Carried him where?'

'Back to us. Soggy left us to find a dog and was injured on the road. It was Conker who carried him back. Conker is a big cat.'

Uimywim swished her fluffy white tail.

'He's the biggest cat I have ever met...'

'I see the soul of every cat,' Uimywim sighed, 'Soggy returned to you, I saw that, but he did not return with any cat.'

'Yes, he did.'

Uimywim held Misty's gaze. 'And you are certain Conker was a cat?'

'Yes,' Misty mewed, 'Conker was a cat. A big cat with long black fur and bright yellow eyes.'

Uimywim shook her head slowly, 'Death takes its toll on the body and the Mind, my old friend, and you have died ... so many times. Soggy has always made friends easily with dogs, so I suspect that he found a dog to carry him back to you. One that looked like a cat.'

'Conker was a cat. A big black cat.'

'Whose soul I cannot see?'

'Perhaps the White Kitten is also going blind with age,' Misty purred.

Uimywim did not purr. She closed her eyes and dimmed her glow, and as the ghosts of the Hill Cats reappeared, she mewed, 'Every Hill Cat that sits before me now, I have met before. I can see the soul of every cat, from their birth to the end of their life. I can find you all. Soggy did not travel with a cat. I am sorry Misty, but your old eyes have deceived you. Your tired mind has confused you, and I cannot again grant you the choice to return to your broken body.'

'I know that!' Misty flicked her tail, 'I accept your invitation, and so do my ghosts. We willingly bring our knowledge to Warkiersu, and with it, the *collective* knowledge that Soggy *was* carried by a cat.'

Winter

'The Hill Cats collected their ghosts?' Nipper woofed, 'Since the first council of Ganlengan? No dog would defy Arlyweh like that. Cats don't like following rules, do they?'

Mellow and Crispy shifted uneasily under the dog's piercing amber stare. Winter pricked her ears. She'd missed Nipper's sharp tongue.

'I don't envy Shadow White,' Nipper went on, 'imagine trying to herd the souls of every cat that ever lived!'

Winter flicked him with her tail, 'I don't think cats want to herd anything.'

'Maybe they should. Plenty of mice in here, you could both practice herding them.'

Mellow purred, 'You want us to waste our time chasing all the mice in this barn into a corner, when we could just steal cheese from the human den, put it in the corner, and sleep while the mice go there themselves?'

Nipper pricked his ears and glanced at Winter, 'Do you think sheep like cheese?'

Winter lolled her tongue, 'We could try. Cats do find interesting ways to avoid following rules.'

The cats purred and the dogs panted as the mice scratched and scurried around under the thick straw in the barn. Winter had found Nipper on a farm high up in the mountains. She'd stayed for a day, and they'd talked about the lives they'd had. But she knew she'd be missed on her own farm. So, they agreed to visit each other every full moon. Nipper had reassured her that he was an expert at escaping, and they would see each other again soon.

When she returned home, Mellow and Crispy were huddled together on a pile of wood beside the barn. Conker and Soggy had sent them to find her, and she had welcomed their company. The cats had settled in well and were enjoying their new lives on the farm, so when Nipper arrived on the full moon, they were all eager to share tales with Red Wind. Nipper was the last to share.

'So, what tale do you want to hear?' he woofed.

Winter licked his ear playfully, 'Tell us the tale of your most difficult escape.'

Nipper whined and turned his head away.

'Sorry,' Winter woofed, 'have I asked for the wrong tale?'

'You asked before Red Wind, so I will tell the tale of the night I escaped the Stepfighters.'

'Stepfighters?' Winter's stomach tightened as she watched the fur rise along Nipper's spine. She'd never known this dog to be afraid of anything.

Nipper growled, 'Dogs who break the rules.'

'Break the rules?' Mellow mewed, 'like ... erm, cats?'

'No, not like cats.' Nipper shook his head, 'You cats do everything in your power to avoid following the rules, but you never truly break them. I'm sure Shadow White has created a thousand worlds with her tears of despair, but you cause no real harm with your actions. These dogs... these soulless dogs break the rules *only* to harm. They do not share tales and they do not surrender. The only commands *they* follow are the ones barked by the cruellest of humans.'

Winter shivered. She couldn't believe that any dog could disrespect Red Wind or refuse a surrender in the name of a Host. 'If this is one of your invisible bones? I'm not digging it up.'

'No.' Nipper licked his lips. 'This is real.'

'So, where are these Stepfighters? I've never heard of such dogs.'

Nipper sat up and growled, 'When they are close, your Listenings will fill with the chaotic haunting messages of the Riddle Dog. No one knows who the Riddle Dog was, or how she died, but every dog who finds meaning in her messages will be driven to despair by her harrowing grief. Every dog, except the Stepfighters I met one night...'

Soggy

'Why you got one eye!' Fizzy woofed.

'I only need one eye to see all your sneaky shenanigans,' Soggy purred.

The little brown puppy yapped and trotted around Soggy, sniffing at his legs. He stopped when he got to his stump of a tail, 'Where it gone?'

'Tails should never be trusted. Tails lie. You should listen to my words.'

'But where is it?'

'The humans at The Sign have it.'

'Why?'

'I don't think they could fix it, so they removed it.'

'Where is it now?'

Soggy took a deep breath and got to his paws, 'Let's look for it. Follow me.' He waited until Fizzy had finished sniffing the grass he'd been sitting on, then headed to the other side of the garden where the little brown puppy had abandoned their new ball.

'You walk funny,' Fizzy woofed as he bounced ahead.

'You be careful, I still have some claws.' Soggy stopped at the edge of the lawn and turned to face the puppy, 'Now listen closely.'

Fizzy flumped down and beat his tail excitedly.

'I am no ordinary cat.'

Fizzy jumped to his paws again and licked Soggy's ear.

Yes, yes, anyway, I am the Warden of Trials, and as such...' he paused to let Fizzy lick his other ear, 'as such, I will now give you your First Trial.'

'What?' Fizzy sat down.

'Your First Trial. Listen closely, then solve the riddle to complete it.'

'Okay!'

'Look now behind you,
'For bouncy bally round thing,
'Stolen from a cat.'

Fizzy turned his head and looked up at the sun.
Soggy sighed, 'Ok ... let's get back to the stick.'